A Parent's Guide To LETTING GO

BETTY FISH, M.S.W.
RAYMOND FISH, Ph.D., M.D.

BETTERWAY PUBLICATIONS, INC.
WHITE HALL, VIRGINIA

Published by Betterway Publications, Inc.
P.O. Box 219
Crozet, VA 22932

Cover and book design by Deborah B. Chappell
Photography by Charles H. Lane
Typography by Chappell Graphics

Library of Congress Cataloging-in-Publication Data

Fish, Betty
  A parent's guide to letting go.

  Includes index.
  1. Teenagers—United States.   2. Parenting—United States.
  3. Separation (Psychology)   I. Fish, Raymond M.   II. Title
HQ796.F59 1988   649'.125   88-2862
ISBN 0-932620-94-9 (pbk.)

Printed in the United States of America
0987654321

Acknowledgments

During the writing of this book, many people were kind enough to read it and offer suggestions. In particular, Suzanne Twohey, M.A., Pamela Soper, M.S.W., and Elaine Jacobson, Ph.D. offered a great deal of support and encouragement.

Additionally, we would like to mention the contribution of Joyce Lohman, Ph.D. and Tim Lohman, Ph.D. Joyce and Tim have been close and encouraging friends throughout this project. It was Joyce and Tim who introduced us to the concept of "Letting Go."

Finally we would like to thank our sons, Bradley and David Fish, who inspired this book by making it unequivocally clear that they were growing up and it was time for us to slowly learn to let go.

Contents

INTRODUCTION

This a book about growth — not just your teen's but also your own personal growth and development. This is a book that intends to challenge you to mature along with your teen. A central idea to bear in mind while reading these pages is that your children's teenage years can be a catalyst for personality changes you, yourself, may need to make as an adult.

If you are experiencing difficulties with your teen, it may be that you are holding on too tightly to your adolescent's life concerns. Many conflicts between teens and their parents revolve around the issue of allowing the teen more control. If the teen is to gain more control, the parent has to learn to LET GO of some controls.

Many problems encountered by parents of teens will be described in this book, but it certainly is not intended as a substitute for counseling. It is a book for parents who are, in some ways, too close to their teens. This book is not for parents who are neglectful of or abusive toward their children; such parents have let go too much.

Normally, letting go is a gradual process which occurs over the years; the pattern should be for parents to lessen controls as teens gain self-control and develop mature judgment. Letting go and relinquishing control can often be a difficult process, however, especially if the parents of the teen are insecure themselves and somewhat uncertain about their own life goals and plans.

Our teens need us to let go so that they can become more independent of us. The aim of this book is to help parents with this often painful process, and to show that the delightful by-product of letting go of other people's worries and problems is that we ourselves can grow. Our lives cease to be lived controlling others, and we can concentrate on ourselves. Difficult — yes. Scary — yes. Painful — indeed. But also exhilarating and liberating.

During the teen years, our children enter a new and exciting phase of their lives. If an adolescent is experiencing difficulty with this developmental change, it may be that we parents are still holding on too tightly to their concerns. By letting go we help not only ourselves, but also our teens by showing them how to become more responsible. No one grows up if someone else is taking care of all their problems. If you want to help your teen to develop and you want to build a stronger sense of your own self, this book offers some suggestions on how to do so.

Chapter One discusses how early influences in the lives of parents can affect their relationship with their teenagers. Many buried feelings from early childhood can surface for parents at the same time their teens begin their own separation process. When parents are unaware that this is happening, it can create all sorts of problems. This chapter is written in the hope that as parents become more aware of the painful forces from the past that can contribute to their current difficulties, they will tolerate their present struggles better.

Chapter Two describes some of the losses and fears that parents frequently experience when their kids hit the teen years. The old family ways of doing things usually change. Children often want to be with their parents less and on their own more. Parents may become fearful and anxious about these changes. This chapter discusses the very normal responses parents might have in such situations.

Just as Chapter Two focuses on helping parents to understand and accept the many emotional changes and feelings that they will likely experience during this time, Chapter Three offers a perspective from the teen's viewpoint. This is a frightening time that will hold many conflicts for teens who, like their parents, suffer fears and losses. This chapter will help parents understand their teen's struggles.

The teen years can be years of personality growth as well as years of loss for both you and your teen — but before there can be growth and change there must be loss. The teen years are often a time of loss of identity, when both parents and teens may well ask, Who am I now? Although this identity crisis is more dramatic in the teen, it can be equally acute for the parent. Both parents and teens go through a natural mourning process, which is described in Chapter Four, along with a discussion of some of the difficulties that may occur if this process is not fully experienced.

Letting go of your teen's responsibilities and accepting changes in your family life are not easy tasks. It can be especially difficult if one does not have a strong sense of self-identity outside the role of parent. The stresses parents go through as their child matures into an adolescent may also intensify if there has been loss in other relationships. This might be loss of a parent's mother or father due to death or continuing relationship difficulties. Single parents who have not resolved the pain of divorce or death of a spouse, as well as parents in marital relationships that are chronically unsatisfying, may find it especially hard to let go of their teen. Chapter Five discusses ways of strengthening one's sense of self so that letting go can become easier and less threatening. Various methods to help parents deal with loneliness and successfully make new attachments as their children need less constant care are also explored here.

Troublesome behavior is a major factor that makes it harder to let go of a teenager. Teens may act up because they want more freedom; paradoxically, however, it becomes more difficult to let go of a teen who is irresponsible. Parents often find themselves engaged in continuous battles or power struggles, and as the difficult behavior escalates, parents find themselves involved more (rather than less) in the teen's life. Chapter Six helps parents assess the level of compliant behavior they are getting from their teen. This book does not suggest any one method of discipline for adolescents. Instead, we suggest that you assess how well your teen is cooperating and then apply certain disciplinary strategies depending on the type of behavior your teen is demonstrating. All these strategies have a common theme. Whether your teen is a straight A student or recently has been put on probation for shoplifting, we suggest letting go and permitting the teen to assume more and more responsibility for his or her behavior. The information in Chapters Two through Six will help you with discipline. None of the numerous books on teen discipline will be helpful, however, if parents do not feel a strong sense of their own values and personal self-worth.

Chapter Seven offers a case illustration of parents who had to learn to let go of their teen's difficulties. In this example we study the case of Pete, who is representative of hundreds of thousands of today's teens. Pete's situation became a crisis before his parents were able to overcome their fears of letting go.

This chapter provides methods parents can use to build the

self-confidence they need to help them let go. Strategies are suggested for dealing with difficult behavior in teens that produce a stronger sense of self in both parent and teen. At this point, it would seem that any problems would be solved, right?

Unfortunately, even when you, as a parent, make constructive changes and begin to let go, society may not support you and your attempts to deal with your teen. Chapter Eight describes some of the societal systems that you may have to deal with once you begin to let go of your involvement in areas that are your teen's concern. There is a good chance you may have to deal with the school system, the mental health system, and the legal system. These systems may undermine your letting-go efforts because they may not be as concerned as you are about the long-range best interests of your child. On the other hand, they can be a tremendous source of help and support. This chapter offers some suggestions for dealing with the various institutions that interact with you and your teen.

The final chapter deals with the legal system. As a parent, you have certain rights and responsibilities. Sometimes the law does not always act in your teen's best interests and your parental aspirations (i.e., helping your teen mature into a responsible adult). It is important to become aware of some of the most pressing issues in juvenile law. It is helpful to know to what extent the law will allow you to let go if you are experiencing major problems with your teen.

This book does not advocate an abrupt and angry letting-go of your teen's life issues. Teens need guidance and appropriate controls, which are lessened as the teen demonstrates increasingly responsible behavior. Letting go can be the key that will help you, the parent, successfully negotiate these transitional years. Letting go is necessary so that your teen can grow. Letting go is essential so that you can continue to grow. Your teen's mounting surge towards independence will challenge you to make some changes. This book attempts to help you meet those challenges.

Good luck!

(By the way, we would like to hear how things have gone for you. If you have any suggestions relevant to the ideas expressed in this book, please drop us a note at Box 3038, Urbana, IL 61801.)

Betty and Raymond Fish

1 Your Childhood Influences How You Deal With Your Teen

"If a mother respects both herself and her child from his very first day onward, she will never need to teach him respect for others. He will, of course, take both himself and others seriously — he couldn't do otherwise. But a mother, who as a child, was herself not taken seriously by her mother as the person she really was will crave this respect from her child as a substitute; and she will try to get it by training him to give it to her — period. The tragic fate that is the result of such training and 'respect' is described in this book.
— *Prisoners of Childhood by Alice Miller, 1981*

Respect the Child Within You

This book will first, help you to think about the changes going on within yourself and your teen, then offer suggestions on how to deal with difficulties in letting go or managing your teen's behavior. These may seem rather cold and intellectual, not unlike a cookbook with the ingredients for a troubled relationship or a road map of directions for change. You may be protesting, "I know family changes during the teen years are important and so are skills for making this time easier, but you just don't understand my pain. Why am I having such a hard time? I feel ridden with guilt because my family is having difficulties; I feel unsure of myself and my place in the world with all these changes in my life. I feel threatened by the loss of my child's love and I don't understand why this is happening. I have tried and tried to do my best, and it's not easy. As a matter of fact, although my mind tells me that it's reasonable and

11

useful to do many of the things suggested in this book, a part of me finds this very difficult and threatening. I don't understand this part of me that is so scared and so lost right now."

This scared and lost part of yourself needs to be heard! We are suggesting that you pay attention to this part — listen to and respect this part of you that does feel needy, alone, and threatened. Indeed, it is this scared part of you, if it is listened to, that can lead the way in helping you and your teen grow. Your teen has a scared, insecure, needy part also. If you allow that part of yourself to be recognized, it may give your child the courage to get to know this part of him or herself as well. It is only when the child within us (scared and insecure) is recognized, that we can begin to truly see what is happening between ourselves and our teen. Similarly, if you are able to recognize and tolerate the part of you that is angry at the conflicts that may be occurring in your family, you may find that you can generate the motivation for following through on some of the ideas in this book. So many of us want to push the sensitive child-like part of us — as well as the angry, hurt part of us — out of awareness.

As you read, you may find yourself having problems following through with some of the suggestions in this book. Don't berate yourself if this occurs. Rather, use this as important information about yourself. What makes it hard for you to do the suggested exercises? Perhaps completion of the exercise might arouse fear or sadness. Instead of ignoring these painful feelings, it is important to recognize them and possibly even discuss them with a therapist, spouse, or trusted friend. Experiencing these feelings is the beginning of the "letting-go process." Remember, this is a gradual process! Don't pressure yourself to do everything in this book or expect perfection from yourself in dealing with your teen. Accept that this process will take time, that you will be making yourself vulnerable, and that you will be experiencing loss. What you are going through is not easy, but the outcome can be positive for you and your teen.

Much of this chapter is based on the book *Prisoners of Childhood* by Alice Miller. In it, the author sensitively portrays how the tragedy of non-acceptance is re-enacted through succeeding generations. If you are willing to focus on your own feelings regarding this transitional time in your life, you will learn much about yourself.

Let's look at some of the ways that the insecure parts of parents' personalities, often covered up and ignored, can contribute to

current difficulties with their teens. How can watching
teens grow stir up long-forgotten emotions?

Unknowingly Using Children to Meet Needs That Were Not Met As Infants

As children, we had an intense need for love and acceptance from
our parents. In most instances, parents do a good enough job of
meeting these needs. Parents are not always perfect and always
available, but they do need to value, love, and protect their
children. A parent's acceptance and dependability should be
conveyed clearly to the child.

Often a child has a parent who loves him or her very much, but
due to certain problems (severe depression, alcoholism, or metal
illness), the parent is unable to communicate this love. Society
often discounts the importance of family life, so much so that a
caring, loving parent may be unable to express love and concern to
a child because the parent is exhausted from work or upset about
having to place the child in inadequate day care facilities. A poig-
nant portrayal by Tillie Olsen shows how a loving, devoted mother
was torn by her need to leave her infant with her only childcare
option — a totally inadequate one.

She was two. Old enough for nursery school, I said, and I did not
know then what I know now— the fatigue of a long day, and the
lacerations of group life in the kinds of nurseries that are only
parking places for children...Except that it would have made no
difference if I had known. It was the only place there was. It was the
only way that we could be together, the only way I could hold a job.
(*Mother to Daughter, Daughter to Mother.*)

Thus, we can see that even if parents have the best intentions
and hopes for relationships with their children, sometimes
economic or emotional problems interfere with fulfillment of a
child's needs.

Some parents' needs were not met as children because their
parents were depressed, alcoholic, or emotionally absent. Such
parents may unconsciously attempt to get their own needs met
through their children. For example, a parent may enjoy a cuddly
infant and later an obedient teen; however, the parent may
withdraw in anger if the infant becomes fussy or the teen becomes
verbally obnoxious. Unconsciously, the parent may have hoped
that the child would fulfill some of the needs for nurturance and

admiration that were not met when the now-parent was growing up. In this sense, parents use their children to meet their own emotional needs. These parents may have a very difficult time with assertive toddlers who love to yell "no"! and demonstrate their independence.

Similarly, for such parents, a child's adolescence can be very traumatic. The toddler's "no" and "mine," as well as a teen's continual absence from home, may seem like rejection to parents who didn't get what they needed in their own childhood. When the parent and teen fight, the parent may associate it with rejection by his own parent during childhood.

Viewing the Present Through Filters from the Past

Other emotional reactions and behaviors the now-parent experienced during childhood may repeat themselves in the current family situation. When individuals' needs are not met in the family of origin, their tendency is to replay earlier, unfinished experiences, unconsciously hoping to resolve earlier events.

For example, Gina grew up in a family with a very depressed mother. Gina's mother was frequently angry and dissatisfied with her life. She often screamed at Gina, and when she became depressed, would withdraw for days at a time. Gina found herself keeping many of her emotional needs unknown, even to herself. To have such needs was dangerous in her family; if she demanded more time with her mother, for example, her mom either got angry or withdrew in hopeless depression. Gina learned not to make demands on her mother, but because Gina's mother had little self-esteem, she tended to demand a lot of Gina in order to bolster her own self-image. Gina's needs took a back seat in her mother's awareness because Gina's mother was so needy herself. Thus, Gina learned that if she wanted to get anything positive from her mother, she had better perform well...if Gina slackened in her performance, her mother withdrew.

Gina experienced her mother as cold, rejecting, and aloof. However, Gina still needed whatever emotional sustenance she could get from her mother, and therefore worked exceedingly hard at covering up her own neediness and anxiety about pleasing her mother. She enacted the role of "super daughter" in her family. Gina's father expected a lot from her because he felt that his wife was emotionally absent, which often made him angry. Gina got into the role of trying to patch up the arguments between her parents. Some of her emotional needs were met by her father when she listened to his complaints against her mother, and she received some additional time from her mother when she complained about Gina's father. Gina attempted to keep conflict to a minimum in her family. She attempted to make things run smoothly and felt it was her fault if things went wrong. She hoped her mother would be pleased with her straight A's in high school and college, and that this would reflect positively on the family.

In the end, Gina paid a price. No one met her emotional needs! She did all the giving. When Gina graduated from college, she met and married a man who was very hard-working and solicitous of her. She loved the attention. However, at the first sign of decreasing attention, she began to panic. She felt as though her husband was withdrawing, just as her mother had. Gina tried harder and harder to stop her husband's perceived withdrawal by working strenuously to be a better wife and mother. She became more and more resentful and wound up feeling exhausted and needy, as she had during childhood. Because of her anger, her husband withdrew even more — thereby perpetuating the cycle of Gina working hard to please him as she had done with her withdrawing parents.

This cycle eventually resulted in growing anger within the marriage, and later, divorce. Gina was pregnant at the time of the divorce and continued to work part-time after the baby (Susie) was born. Gina loved being a mother and felt needed and wanted. Finally Gina felt she had found someone — her loving infant — who would admire her and fill up the empty emotional space inside her. If the baby cried or was upset, Gina would panic, and she began to serve the infant as she had her parents and her husband, fearing the baby's emotional abandonment.

Additionally, Gina did not see Susie as she really was, but instead the tiny child she once was, the child with unmet needs. Thus, Gina continued a pattern of excessive overidentification with and caretaking for Susie, who was never permitted to experience a normal degree of frustration. At times, Gina even saw her own mother in Susie, such as when Susie became (as all babies will) upset and demanding. Although Gina was extremely tied to Susie, she saw the infant through distorted filters from the past.

When Susie became a teen, she began to engage in separation behavior, such as going out frequently and having bad moods.

Gina, who interpreted this conduct as a withdrawal of love, panicked. On an unconscious level, Gina experienced Susie as her withdrawing mother. Continuing in her old pattern, Gina began to serve her perfectly capable teenage daughter inappropriately because she feared losing her love if she didn't. As in her marriage and her family of origin, this caused mounting resentment.

Soon Gina and Susie locked horns. When Gina began to put some appropriate limits on Susie (e.g., curfew, completion of chores, or requirements that she earn her own spending money, Susie appeared sad, hurt, and victimized. Seeing Susie like this really got to Gina because she identified with those same feelings she'd had as a child. As a result, Gina would waiver and drop her rules and requests. Inevitably, Gina wound up doing the chores herself, feeling resentful of Susie's non-compliance with rules.

Conflict increased between mother and daughter. At age sixteen, Susie ran away. Gina again experienced abandonment. However, this time she could not pick herself up and work harder to overcome the situation. She was thrown into an emotional crisis she had forestalled for a long time. The pain overwhelmed her. Years of suppressed grief and anger at not having her own needs met as a child began to emerge when her daughter ran away. This resulted in feelings of profound hopelessness and helplessness over the loss of her parents, husband, and now, child. Gina sought professional help, and fortunately was able to work through her intense feelings of abandonment through therapy.

Replaying Old Roles and Attitudes with Those in the Current Environment

OVER-RESPONSIBLENESS, DISTRUST, AND A SENSE OF ENTITLEMENT

One of the many insights Gina experienced during her therapy sessions is that children who grow up in families like her own often tend to replay the old roles they learned as children. They also carry over many of the characteristic attitudes they experienced as children.

For example, Gina carried over the extreme sense of over-responsibleness for her parents into her marriage and child-rearing. Although it might appear positive to develop such extreme responsibleness and caring as Gina possessed, in reality it is a problem. Children like Gina who are cast into an inappropriate adult role too soon get an exaggerated sense of their own power. They develop a secret internal sense that they are better than others.

Although someone like the adult Gina may appear to be very "giving" to others, underneath she has a secret sense of being superior to the individuals she is giving to. This is reflected in Gina's overdoing for others what they are capable of doing for themselves. While Gina felt superior to her own parents, she also has an exceedingly difficult time trusting family and friends enough to get really close. Although it appears that Gina trusts others, this is superficial. She was not trusted herself as a child. She was accepted only when she fit her parent's view of who they felt she should be: she was not trusted to be "just" a growing little girl. As a result, Gina did not really trust her parents. If she did not perform adequately, she could not rely on their love...neither could she depend upon them for constancy and guidance. Underneath Gina's "giving" to her daughter and husband was the unspoken superiority of "I'm so good to take care of you." Also, there was the unspoken demand of "Since I'm doing so much for you, you owe me and must never abandon me."

Just as Gina was never really sure of her parents' love or her own self-worth, so too was she uncertain of her husband's and daughter's affection. She believed that no one could really love someone as unlovable as herself unless she served them. This old attitude helped to generate resentment on Gina's part, and ultimately the abandonment she feared and expected materialized. Gina's expectations set up a tragic self-fulfilling prophecy.

How Parents' Old Issues Interact with What Their Teen Experiences

Gina saw in her daughter the hurt and needy child she had been herself. This filter so distorted Gina's view of Susie that Gina overprotected a perfectly healthy, capable child and teen. Gina projected her own feelings of sadness onto her daughter and attempted to deal with her own neediness for nurturing by taking excessive care of Susie. This pattern caused problems in adolescence when Gina did not get compliance or help from Susie, whom she had been serving for thirteen years. By the time Gina began to have more mature expectations of Susie as a teen, Susie was already used to being taken care of and having mom feel sorry for her.

The changing expectations on Gina's part as her daughter grew older resulted in conflict. The more Gina and Susie fought (over everything from dishes to smoking marijuana), the more Gina felt abandoned by Susie. Gina began to perceive her daughter as cruel and rejecting, like her own mother, so Gina served her. This caused Gina to withdraw even further from Susie, who in turn became angry at her mother's distancing. When Gina stopped doing everything for her daughter, Susie became even more furious, since she was used to wielding power over her mother. She did not like the new maternal demands about curfew and chores. She acted out even more to retaliate against her mother and to deal with her own anxiety about growing up. When Gina saw Susie acting out (e.g., truancy, increased pot smoking, trashing the house), she began to set even more rules for Susie. She was convinced that Susie needed more and more rules in order to be restrained. However, the more Gina attempted to enforce rules, the more Susie defeated her. Finally, Gina gave in when Susie tried to follow the rules, but just "couldn't remember" most of them. Gina, defeated, reverted to serving Susie — just like she had her mother. Both mother and daughter became negatively dependent on each other.

Even teens who are not acting out to the degree Susie did may trigger old emotional reactions in their parents that spark a cycle of conflict. For some parents who have had little emotional nurturing themselves, normal age-appropriate teen separation can cause panic. Such parents might relate to an independently developing child in the same way as they did to their own emotionally abandoning parents. If parents see their young teen in this light, they will convey their sense of hurt and anger to their child. The child experiences the parent's attitude as "I'm horrible unless I meet my parent's needs and stay dependent on them. If I meet my own needs for growth and independence, then I'm a disgusting individual for abandoning my parents."

Both parents and teens are usually unconscious of these conflicts as they are aware only of the pain they each experience. Like Gina as a teen, some children will deal with this conflict by continuing to serve their parents' emotional needs, thus sacrificing their own growth. Most teens, however, due to the physical and cognitive changes of adolescence, feel an overpowering need to assert their own power and independence. But unless teens feel free to separate and have a history of taking some responsibility for themselves, they may be quite frightened of this new independence they naturally desire. Such teens, like Susie, act out their need to break free of emotionally dependent parents. Rather than experiencing and acknowledging their fears, hurts, and angers, they avoid facing them and act out these feelings through drugs, promiscuity, and antisocial behavior.

This acting out behavior is often a response to parental withdrawal of affection as the teen begins to emotionally separate, combined with the teen's own feelings of separation and aloneness that come with entering a new stage of development.

Feelings of Self-Loathing Contribute to Conflicts with the Teen

Buried very deeply in their psyche, people who grew up in homes like Gina's may have a sense of being bad and disgusting. Gina truly felt she was a poisonous person, although she worked hard to cover up these feelings by overly caring for others. Therefore, when her daughter became a teen and started to appropriately separate, Gina suspected the worst in Susie, just as she secretly suspected the worst from herself. Teens of insecure parents like Gina sense this negative expectation in their parents. And often they live up to the negative expectations. Gina had little trust in her daughter because underneath she had little trust in herself. Gina attempted to tightly control every aspect of her daughter's life because she did not really trust her daughter to have her own internal controls. Gina's daughter rebelled at these controls, further confirming her mother's distrust. Again, Gina was replaying occurrences in her own childhood with her daughter. Just as Gina's mother did not trust Gina — withdrawing unless Gina behaved perfectly— Gina did not trust Susie.

This negative expectation cycle of the generations tends to perpetuate itself. Gina felt terrified (just as her own mother did) if Susie did not behave ideally, because that made her look bad. It was as though Susie's negative behavior would expose the imperfections that Gina was trying so hard to conceal. Sensing her mother's desperation for her to act perfectly, Susie used her negative behavior as a weapon. By getting into all sorts of trouble, Susie could get back at her mother for her distrust and lack of acceptance of the normal mistakes of growing up. Just as Gina expected the worst from her daughter, Susie was on the lookout to show the imperfections in Gina. Although it is common for teens to begin to notice the shortcomings of their parents and to be angry that the

once-idealized parent has clay feet, this was much more pronoun-
ced in Gina's daughter. Because she did not feel accepted when
she made errors, Susie was determined to "expose" her mother's
imperfections as well. She was on the lookout for any mistakes her
mother made, gleefully pointing them out to Gina. By the time
Susie was thirteen, mother and daughter were in a mutually destructive game of attempting to expose each other's inadequacies.
Deep down, both longed for love and acceptance. But feeling an
absence of respect, each became enraged and reacted by attack
and withdrawal.

Resolving Parental Problems
Through the Teen

When children are growing up, they experience a variety of
emotions. These feelings vary from intense need for closeness to
absolute rage if they feel abandoned. Envy is another emotion frequently experienced by children. Envy and rage may be
particularly prevalent in children who are deprived of parental
nurturance for whatever reason. Children longing for needed
parental responsiveness and attunement may feel an insatiable
internal demand for such nurturance. By the same token, the
emotionally absent parent frequently resents the child's demands
and withdraws from the child. The young child then becomes even
more needy of affection.

Ironically, an attempt to get these needs met might result in
withdrawal. Thus, the child of such parents might stop asking to
have needs met. The child may even deny the experience of having needs. This was the case with Gina. She did not recognize the
needy little child in herself. She only saw herself as an exceptionally competent and giving person. However, she was ultra-
sensitive to the little child in her young daughter, who she saw as
being fragile, sad, and hurt. When her daughter was nine years old,
Gina was still doing tasks for her that a child of nine could
easily handle.

Gina projected her own unmet needs and sadness onto her
daughter, as well as long-forgotten hurts about her lack of
emotional nurturance when she was a child. Instead of feeling her
own pain, Gina projected that pain onto her child. Thus, she took
care of what she perceived as her sad, needy little girl, when what
she really needed to do was to take care of her own needs and not

overdo for her capable child.

Just as Gina saw in her daughter the neediness that she felt within herself, so too did she attribute impulses of disorderliness and feelings of being out of control to her daughter that really were within her. Since Gina had to be the "ideal" child for her parents, she had to deny consciousness of many emotions that would have brought her into conflict with her parents. For example, Gina was never a messy child. This was prohibited. She was always expected to maintain strict limits for herself. Internally Gina resented these rigid controls and felt very much out of control; very often she felt like giving in to what she saw as laziness or rule-breaking. But she fought off these impulses. Pushing these thoughts out of awareness, she projected them onto her daughter. She became very rigid with Susie, demanding strict order and rule-keeping with no exceptions. Again, Gina was projecting onto her daughter what she felt inside — disorder and chaos. She attempted to control the disorder she saw in her daughter: cleaning her room and over-organizing aspects of her daughter's life that should have been of no concern to Gina. The mother's internal state was played out with the daughter in the mother's role. Unfortunately, just as Susie became untrustworthy and immature in response to her mother's expectations, so did she also become disorderly and out of control.

Gina's desperate attempts to be a good, kind, and concerned parent were often undermined by unresolved pain from her own childhood. Gina grew up with a demanding mother who had little regard for Gina's internal world of feelings. What was important was that Gina reflected positively on the family and served her parents' needs. Even when Gina left her family of origin, her mother's expectations stayed with her in her head. When her mother was no longer making demands, Gina played out this drama with her husband and later her child. The parts of Gina's world that were unacknowledged (e.g., her pervasive feelings of self-loathing and distrust, her own infantile neediness, her feelings of disorder and chaos) were all seen in her daughter, but not herself. Because of unawareness of these aspects of herself, Gina viewed her daughter with a destructive filter.

Over time, Gina's distrust, disappointment, and anger at her daughter became a self-fulfilling prophecy. Indeed, her daughter had behaved as Gina expected. At thirteen she was not trustworthy, had no internal controls on her behavior, and was indifferent to her mother's feelings. She acted like the sad, helpless infant that Gina had projected onto her. She made constant demands on her mother. When she ran away, Gina felt abandoned. The drama had played its final act. Susie now played the role Gina's mother had played when Gina was a child. Gina perceived her as being demanding and abandoning; however, she was still desperate for her daughter's love, just as she had been for her mother's.

With hard work and much pain in therapy, Gina was able to re-own those parts of herself that she had projected onto her daughter. Gina no longer served anyone but her own best interests. Additionally, once Gina began to see her daughter with clearer vision, the two of them could move closer. Indeed, once Susie disengaged from the power struggle with her mother, she began to look at her own distortions of Gina. In order to let go of her teen, Gina had to take the preliminary exceedingly difficult and painful task of letting go of past issues with her own mother.

What Can Be Learned From Gina's Story

Gina's story was told in order to relate how complicated and confusing the letting go process can be — especially if there are unresolved issues in the life of the parent of a teen. In addition, Gina's story is intended to encourage parents to be compassionate toward their own histories of pain and loss. Letting go is much more difficult if one has experienced a great deal of abandonment, as Gina did.

Gina's story also shows that parents who care desperately about their children can still have intense family conflict and not even understand why it is happening. This can occur despite concerted efforts to be a good parent. These same issues could have played themselves out even if Gina were still married, although the stronger the marital bond, the less chance these old needs will be replayed through the children.

Finally, Gina's story emphasizes the difficulty of the letting go process. So, if the techniques in this book seem too difficult to fulfill or too simplistic for your situation, consider professional help. Remember, too, if you are feeling scared, hurt, confused, and sad, you owe it to yourself to listen to and respect these feelings!

2 Parental Emotions Associated with Letting Go

What can I say, but that it's not easy?
I cannot lift the stones out of your way,
And I can't cry your bitter tears for you.
I would if I could, but what can I say?

But we're not one, we're worlds apart.
You and I,
Child of my body, bone of my bone
Apple of my eye.

Rosalie Sorrels, Poet

In a sense the young child you have known for a dozen years may seem at times to have died. Just as a caterpillar dies so that a butterfly may emerge, a part of a child seems to die when he or she turns into a teenager. Still, teens are often childlike when it comes to issues of responsibility. This makes letting go more difficult: teens want respect and privileges, but often do not acknowledge the accompanying responsibility. Teens want it both ways, and their parents often seem to as well.

You may have ambivalent feelings about your child growing up. Although you may be delighted to see your child maturing, part of you may be experiencing sadness and uncertainty regarding this new stage in your child's life. These feelings are a signal that a new stage in your own life has begun.

You may be surprised to find yourself experiencing sadness and fears, along with pride, in your child's growth. You need to recognize and mourn the loss of your "little one" and realize that now you have a "big one." Both you and your child are in a transition period. You will likely have feelings of loss and uncertainty coupled with feelings of admiration about your child's development and changes. Until you recognize and deal with your ambivalent emotions, you may be too distracted and upset to use the self-help techniques listed in the following chapters.

This chapter will help you understand the many losses, fears, and emotional changes you may experience during your child's teenage years. Once you recognize the shifts from the past, it will be easier to accept and mourn the losses, face the fears, and help yourself adjust to your new situation. Later chapters in this book tell you how to do each of these things. This is not just a time of loss. Your child's adolescence provides an opportunity for you to grow also.

Personal Losses	Losses Related to the Child
Youth	Dependency of the Child
Sexual abilities	Daily routine of caring for child
Athletic abilities	Control over the child
Unfulfilled career ambitions	Family activities and routines
Physical attractiveness	Ability to make choices for child
One's own parents	Illusion of being able to plan child's life

Table 2-1. Losses Some Parents Believe They Experience As Their Teens Grow

Parent's Personal Losses

Just when teens are at the peak of their physical attractiveness, parents are usually losing their youth. Parents, often striving to make ends meet, may feel exhausted, depleted of physical and emotional energy. Parents may experience demands from their teens, their other children, their own parents, and their jobs. Worry about future financial burdens and health problems sometimes leads to chronic tiredness and premature aging.

Some parents feel the excitement fading from their own sexual relationships at this time. The adolescent's newly emerging sexuality may be quite threatening in these families. Parents may become jealous as their teens develop intimate emotional and possibly sexual relationships with others. At the same time the intensity and frequency of sex may be decreasing in the parents' relationships, it may be at its peak for the teen.

Parents may feel that they are losing their physical attractiveness. Again, this perceived loss may be intensified by parents comparing themselves to their curvaceous or muscular teen. The majority of adults in this country have a steady decline in their physical condition and athletic ability from the age of twenty-five until they die. Parents may have been watching their child's baseball games and driving carpools in their spare time instead of exercising. In such cases, parents may feel angry and cheated if the teen makes certain decisions, such as to drop out of sports. Parents can make constructive use of their anger by focusing on their own health and physiques, and by letting go of concerns regarding the teen's athletic abilities. The parent may do better to quit worrying about a teen who decides not to be on the football team. Instead, the parent can take out a membership for himself or herself in a local gym.

Parents may feel that their own career ambitions have not been fulfilled. Their disappointment may be highlighted as they watch their adolescent excitedly begin to chart educational or career plans. The parent may have put off or given up career plans so that the child could live in the best neighborhood, go to the best schools, and have the best shot at a good career. This is the "I wanted my children to have everything I could not" syndrome. Feelings of disappointment, panic, and resentment are to be expected if the teen rejects parentally-approved career opportunities. For example, one father spent many hours a week tutoring his daughter so that she could do well in an advanced high school program. The father wanted his daughter to be able to go to a good college, partly because of frustrations with his own career. The girl decided she was not interested in the extra work demanded by the college preparatory program. Soon the father was spending more time on U.S. history than the daughter, trying to get her to learn the material. Study sessions turned into arguments over how much time the daughter had actually spent on her instruction. The father resented his daughter's lack of motivation. Finally, the father let go: he let the daughter take responsibility for her own grades and school study program. He did not force her to study. Although this young woman decided she did not want to begin college in the near future, the responsibility for this decision was put where it belonged: on her. The father stopped worrying and stopped wasting time and effort on a futile attempt to make his daughter prepare for a college career she didn't want. Instead, he began to make important career changes for the only person he really had control over: himself. He had to learn to mourn the loss of his dreams for his daughter's career. He learned to resume his own life goals. He also learned to value and enjoy his own achievements.

While you are busy dealing with your teenager, it's quite possible your own parents may have health problems. At the mid-point of life, many people must come to grips with the serious decline in health or the actual loss of a parent. Your parents, on whom you depended for so many years, might be dead now or increasingly dependent upon you. You may become painfully aware of your own separateness and mortality, as your own parents age and your teens move away. You may develop what has been called "an existential sense of your aloneness." You realize that you no longer have parents who can care for you as actively as in the past. Your child has his or her own life to live. You really are alone and responsible for yourself. This sense of aloneness, which can be exacerbated by the death of one's parents, can be quite frightening and painful for those who have always been dependent upon, or surrounded by, family. Experiencing this feeling of aloneness can cause a major crisis for some people.

Parent's Losses Related to the Child

LOSS OF DEPENDENCY OF THE CHILD

The old parent-child guiding relationship you had with your child will change considerably or even seem to be lost entirely as your teen grows up. The close, dependent family ties you felt for years may seem to disintegrate. At this time, parents often experience loss of illusions regarding the nature of family life. Many of us harbor secret illusions that our families will turn out just like the Waltons or the crew on "Father Knows Best." When our own John Boy is discovered with a joint or other drugs, we may feel furious because of the teen's action and also because our dream of perfect family life has been shattered. If our children have values or lifestyles at variance with our own, we may feel a major loss. We may also feel intense guilt, assuming, "If only we were better parents... then the dream of our ideal family life would have been realized." Single parents are apt to blame ANY problems which arise on their failure to have a spouse or on their inability to give as much time to the children as two parents could. Such reasoning is false and unfair to the single parent.

Loss of the Daily Routine of Caring for the Child

Parents often feel guilty when they are not in the familiar, comfortable routine of constantly doing things for their children. All of a sudden the teen will want to choose clothes, ride with friends, and engage in activities without you. It is not unusual for a parent to feel unneeded and useless because he or she is not constantly occupied by taking care of the children. Some parents misinterpret their teen's newfound independence as a rejection of parental caring and love. The teen's independence is not rejection; it is a sign of a parenting job well-done. It is often best to let your teen make decisions, gradually assume responsibility for personal affairs, and make some mistakes in life. Do not misinterpret your teen's normal and healthy activities of seeking independence as a decrease in love or caring.

Sometimes the loss of family routine is due in part to the teen's new schedule. For example, Sunday breakfast may no longer be a family affair simply because the teen wants to sleep late. Parents may find it useful to establish new family rituals which do fit the teen's schedule, such as having regular family Sunday lunches or dinners. If the teen is simply not interested in family activities at any time, parents may find it useful to plan and enjoy activities which do not include the teen. For example, parents can plan to go out to dinner every Sunday night with an interesting couple. A single parent might take the teen's independence as a reminder that the teen is growing up and away. This might motivate the single parent to resume dating. At the very least, single parents will be able to spend time with others their own age without the guilt sometimes associated with "leaving the children alone."

LOSS OF CONTROL OVER THE TEEN

Normally, a teen takes control of his or her own life gradually, over several years. The teen makes more and more decisions, and the parents gradually lose control over issues in the teen's life. Thus, letting go becomes a gradual process. Let go of your teen, even when you are certain the teen is making minor mistakes. Use your time to develop your own interests. For example, if your teen has final examinations coming up and decides not to study, let the teen feel the results of not studying when grades come out. It is better to learn this in high school than to flunk out of college or to do poorly in a job. Some parents try to tutor their children, making sure they "learn enough." These children do not learn the important lessons that come with failure. And, the parent loses valuable time. Rather than try to force the teen into unwanted study periods, the parent would do better to read that book there was never time for, go to a movie, or do some exercise. A decrease of focus on the child will help both the parent and the teen grow. A parent who continues to be overly concerned about every aspect of the teen's life must ask, "Why am I holding on so tightly? What's in it for me? Am I doing so much for my teenager in order to satisfy some need of my own? What area in my own life is being neglected or avoided because I am so closely focused on my child?"

When a teen does schoolwork, encouragement and help (when it is asked for) are appropriate. However, the teen will eventually decide how seriously studies will be taken. Some parents feel the loss of the familiar role of "supervisor." Less time is spent with the teen, and there is less control over the teen. The acquisition of self-control is normal and necessary if the teen is to grow. Many parents say, "If I were you, I would study for that test tomorrow." The teen, on the other hand, may feel that other things are more important. School grades, wanting to get into college, not being able to get a job, or embarrassment in class may provide sufficient motivation for study, but repeated reminders or arguments from parents often leads to nothing more than prolonged fights.

Such long-term arguments are sometimes referred to as "power struggles." Some teens will do poorly in school (or get into various kinds of trouble) in order to get back at parents for real or imagined wrongs. This is referred to as revenge. Other teens try to control their parents through the threat of poor schoolwork or other undesirable behavior. This is a form of control. An effective way to deal with power struggles, revenge, and control is to realize that the issues involved are the teen's problems and not yours. School grades, for example, should be the concern of the teen. Let the teen's appearance be his or her concern. Do not try to control the teen's grades, looks, dress, or other personal items which do not affect you or others directly. In other words, LET GO. Later chapters in this book offer suggestions on how to accomplish this change in your behavior. Many attempts at controlling the behavior of teens backfire. You can, however, control your own behavior, including how you react to your teen. For example, you need not take your poorly-dressed teen to a fancy restaurant.

These ideas may seem radical to you. You may feel that letting go like this will leave you powerless and without control. In fact, this book repeatedly illustrates how letting go can lead to increased parental power and a new sense of self-control. One of the reasons a parent (or anyone) tries to control others is that they feel out of control in their own lives. By attempting to control another individual, people feel more powerful. Pervasive feelings of insecurity and lack of self-assertion are temporarily assuaged as they begin to feel empowered by ordering another individual's life. Parents who are not experiencing and expressing their own personal power may attempt to gain power by controlling a spouse or child. This may work until a spouse becomes more assertive, or until a child becomes an adolescent. At this time, many parents are put into crisis. The old ways of ordering another's life will no longer be accepted by the controlled spouse or teen.

Chapters Four and Five offer suggestions for dealing with this frightening situation of no longer being able to control someone else. This situation often results in an identity crisis. If feelings of insecurity and lack of control are not dealt with constructively, they may be (and often are) dealt with destructively. Parents threatened with loss of control may begin to drink, overeat, or engage in other compulsive behavior. If a parent refuses to let go of the developing teen and face this personal crisis, the teen may develop pathological responses to the controlling parent. For example, the teen may drink excessively, use drugs, become depressed, or develop an eating disorder.

Paradoxically, this type of behavior is a cry for independence and personal power from the teen, as well as a form of punitive control against the parent who won't let go. Parents can be driven to distraction by anorexics who won't eat, bulimics who eat too much, and druggies who need constant watching. A vicious cycle is set in motion. The parent wants to control the teen; in response, the teen develops problems, and thereby winds up controlling the parent. No one lets go.

LOSS OF FAMILY ACTIVITIES AND ROUTINES

Problems associated with vacations and free time can also shatter your illusions of togetherness and control over family members. Activities that previously took up much of your time may be lost. Family activities that previously involved the child may no longer be appreciated. The child who once pleaded to go to ball games is no longer interested. The once enthusiastic traveler is now totally indifferent or even hostile to any family vacation. Parents may feel a loss of family structure and meaning. The child is no longer part of the parent's routine. The child is no longer the center of the parent's life. Instead of driving to the beach with you for the weekend or for your summer vacation, your teen may prefer to stay with a friend. If you force your teen to come with you on vacation, you may have a miserable time. The teen may resist being cast in the child role.

In the teen years it is often more realistic to forget "togetherness" and try for understanding, respect, and a live-and-let-live attitude. It is often helpful to begin to treat your teen as you would a respected friend rather than a child. After all, you would not demand that a friend accompany you on a vacation or outing. Togetherness often becomes an unrealistic goal as the teen becomes a more mature, separate person. You must give up your yearning for being with the teen as much as was previously possible. Realize that this is normal and healthy (within reasonable limits). Realize it is not unusual to experience feelings of resentment, guilt, and sadness when spending less time with your child. But, realize also that it is healthy for the teen to separate from you. And recognize that you can use the new free time to LIVE. Later chapters will tell you how to make these role changes into a constructive opportunity for yourself.

In single-parent families it often seems that the child is, of necessity, encouraged to become more independent and make more decisions before adolescence. Some of the daily routines and family activities enjoyed before adolescence in two-parent families may never be experienced. Therefore, single parents are sometimes especially fearful and sad about letting go "too soon."

LOSS OF THE ABILITY TO MAKE CHOICES FOR THE TEEN, ESPECIALLY CAREER AND LIFE PLANS

We have been discussing loss of control over various aspects of the teen's life. At first teens make day-to-day choices concerning dating, neatness, and athletics. Later, they begin to make choices that affect their careers. When the parents see their teen making choices that adversely affect the teen's future career, they sometimes try to intervene. Loss of control over the teen's day-to-day activities is often associated with a loss of control over long-term career plans. For example, Don found some of his high school classes boring. Don's father suggested that Don sign up for different classes, or just put up with the situation, as a good school record was required for college. Instead of making an effort to change classes, Don started to skip his classes. He asked his parents to give him excuses for being absent from school: he was sick, he had a dentist appointment, he missed his bus, he had to run errands. Sometimes Don got excuses from his mother. Sometimes he got them from his father. Sometimes he forged them or just did not bother to get an excuse. Eventually, Don was found walking the streets during school hours by the police. When his father, mother, and school counselor put the entire picture together, it became clear that Don had been truant much more than anyone had suspected. Because of Don's now obvious pattern of deliberately lying to get out of classes, his parents insisted that the school not excuse him from making up missed work. Don would have to decide if he wanted to do the work to succeed in school or not.

This example illustrates how letting go of a teen's behavior (while encouraging the school system to follow through with the consequences) can help parents become more powerful.

When a teen walks or sneaks out of the house after being grounded, parents often feel a loss of control. If a teen lands in jail, parents may feel that years of investment in building the child's career and the possibility of a future life of interaction with the child have been lost.

For example, a thirteen-year-old may be grounded for an infraction of family rules. He goes to his room, climbs out of the window, and sneaks off to play with his friends. The episode is symbolic of the loss involved in this developmental stage. The parent's needs for importance and control by fulfilling the role of disciplinarian for the child are frustrated. By climbing out of the window, the adolescent is sending the message that the old ways of relating to the parent must change. The teen is demanding more control and power. The parent's needs for fulfillment in these areas must be satisfied in some other way. The parents must mourn the loss of control over the teen. The parents must redefine their role and develop new modes of responses to and discipline of the teen. Parents must find new ways to fulfill their need for importance, self-esteem, and control. These are certainly losses for the parent, but they are also an opportunity for new growth.

Similarly, as a child, the adolescent met his needs for security and belonging by following parental directives. As an adolescent, he attempts to meet these needs through his peer group. This adolescent, who may be wanting more control in family decision-making, must be helped to fulfill needs for belonging and control in positive, socially acceptable ways within the peer group and the family.

Another example of loss of parental control involves a fourteen-year-old girl. Her parents were upset when, after seven years of piano lessons, she emphatically refused to practice. Her parents experienced hurt and loss. There were battles over the teen's piano playing. These parents were feeling hurt for several reasons. They had hoped that their daughter might consider a career in music. Second, they had hoped to continue to be guides and mentors for their daughter's music. Thus, they also felt the loss of a role. Another loss concerned the very practical area of money. They had looked upon their daughter's lessons and the purchase of a piano as a financial investment. They came to view this as a waste of money. Being music lovers, these parents felt that their daughter was rejecting their values. Finally, they became constantly embattled with their daughter. The little girl, who once complied willingly and idealized her parents, now appeared to be furious at them. Thus, most crucially, these parents came to fear a loss of their daughter's love.

Normal Mourning	Abnormal Mourning
1. Some denial	1. Excessive denial
2. Sadness	2. Unexpressed anger
3. Anger	3. Depression
4. Ambivalent feelings	4. Guilt
5. Acceptance	5. Unresolved ambivalent feelings
	6. Failure to accept the teen as a separate individual

Table 2-2. Emotions Associated With Losses: Mourning and Bereavement

---

Fear of the losses listed in Table 2-1.

Fear of the loss of love
Fear of the unknown
Fear for the child's physical safety
Fear of not fitting society's image of the Good Parent
Fear of not knowing what to do if not parenting

Table 2-3. Fears Associated With Letting Go

Fears Associated With Letting Go

The threat of loss may cause the emotional response of fear and anxiety. What follows are some common fears of parents during their children's adolescence. These fears make it more difficult for the parent to "let go".

The threat of the losses listed in Table 2-1 may cause parents to become fearful and anxious. The fears may cause the parent to hold on tighter and prevent letting go. One may fear a specific thing or event. For example, the parent may fear the teen's drinking, driving, or using pot (marijuana). Anxiety comes from a less well-defined problem: the threat of loss of identity (i.e., not knowing what to do if you are not parenting), the feeling that things are not right, or a general feeling of uncertainty about the future.

FEAR OF LOSS OF LOVE

Parents may fear loss of the child's love and respect. When parents feel threatened by the loss of their child's love and loss of their self-esteem (which is based on being a parent), they often respond by blaming or withdrawing. Blaming and distancing are two defense mechanisms that prevent one from experiencing the painful emotions associated with loss. These mechanisms attempt to prevent the painful emotions of depression and mourning that normally accompany the loss of someone or something important. Blaming and distancing are ways of denying sadness, short-circuiting the task of mourning, which, as will be explained in later chapters, is a necessary part of letting go.

You may find yourself constantly blaming, or angrily emotionally withdrawing (distancing) from your teenager. You may be avoiding the necessary letting go process (and the accompanying painful feelings) by engaging in escalating power struggles with your teen. Fighting with your teen causes you to continue to hold on, worsens the uncertainty associated with loss of control, and delays the experiences of mourning and sadness which are necessary for letting go.

Frequent arguments over practically any issue can continue the unproductive, clinging behavior of both the teen and parent. At the same time, the parent is not allowing the teen to take charge of his or her own life. For example, the teen does not learn self-control and responsibility, and the parent may spend many tense hours unproductively, when there are repeated or prolonged discussions about schoolwork, hair styles, dress, choice of friends, or participation of the teen in family activities. Frequent arguments between a teen and parent signal difficulty with the letting go process. The fighting, although painful, keeps the parents and teen over-involved in each others' lives.

Some parents are so fearful of loss of a child's love that they give into their adolescent's every demand. Some parents feel a loss of love when the teen spends more time away from home and takes less part in family activities. This is normal, average teenage behavior. Also, when religious and social values are questioned by the teen, some parents feel that they and their values are being rejected. They fear the teen will stop loving or even caring about them. At this point, it is important that the parents examine and uphold their own moral values. To compromise your values as a favor to your teen will cause the teen to lose respect for you. Love grows out of respect. Love is likely to be destroyed when self-respect is lost. The questioning of parental values by teens can motivate parents to examine and clarify their own thinking.

Fear of loss of a teen's love makes the parent very vulnerable to blackmail by the teen. The parent may be hesitant to set and enforce limits because of an underlying fear that the teen may reject the limits. Teens learn to manipulate fearful parents by implying that love will be withheld if demands are not met. These teens may escalate their demands and demonstrate intolerable behavior. Sometimes teens secretly hope that their parents will stand up for their own values and rights and set appropriate limits. When parents fail to respond firmly to unreasonable demands and intolerable behavior, teens often feel guilty. Teens in this situation tend to become fearful of growth and become even more tied to their parents.

Some parents may attempt to insure their child's continuing love by constantly buying the teen material items. Fear of loss of love and other fears make the parent *HOLD ON TIGHTER* to the child rather than *LET GO*.

Parents often fear losing their teen's love if they set limits on their behavior; it is difficult for them to be assertive with someone who is important to them. Often such parents grew up in families where they were fearful of being rejected if they failed to serve their own parents by always being the super-responsible and giving person in the family. They have carried this pattern over from their own families of origin to the families they have created. Rescuing and taking care of other people has almost become an automatic role.

Rescuing other people provides rescuers with two types of rewards. First, rescuers are so busy taking care of others that there is no time to look at their own pains and troubles. Often such individuals think that their spouses, friends, or children are very sad and in need of constant support. What is actually happening is that the rescuer is thinking that others are feeling the sadness that he or she is feeling inside. When rescuers think they see pain in others, they are often projecting their own sadness onto others. The second reward for rescuers is the hope that they will keep the other individual close or dependent by taking care of them. An example would be a parent who takes over chores that a teen could easily handle without assistance. Such a parent may be attempting to ward off the fear that the teen will abandon the parent as the teen matures. This is often not a conscious act on the part of the parent. Such parents were often sensitized to emotional abandonment in their own childhoods. Teens sense this fear of loss of love in their parents and may exploit it to get what they want.

FEAR OF THE UNKNOWN

Parents have fears regarding their changing family and its members. Parents often fear the unfamiliar situations and unknown factors that come with the teen years. Difficult questions arise: "How am I going to related to this changed individual?" "Can I handle all the difficulties of parenting a teen?" "Will my kid do anything to get me or himself in trouble?" "Have I done okay as a parent up until now?" "What will the future hold for me now that my child is older?"

FEAR FOR THE CHILD'S SAFETY

Fear for the teen's physical safety becomes a concern and may become an area of parental vulnerability. For example, a parent may drive the teen around town in the middle of the night because it is considered unsafe to walk or take a cab. Many teens do things to injure themselves and others: drugs, reckless driving, promiscuous sexual activity, drinking, and fighting are common examples.

FEAR OF NOT FITTING SOCIETY'S IMAGE
OF THE GOOD PARENT

Fear of contradicting societal expectations of being a good parent sometimes keeps parents from letting go. Regardless of the teen's behavior, parents often feel obligated to supply a healthy allowance, nice clothes, use of the car and telephone, and chauffeur service. Breaking this cycle of self-sacrifice can force a teen to assume more responsibility and force parents to find new meaning in their own lives. Parents may face many embarrassing questions: "What will others say if our teen's clothes are not the best ?" "Will other people think I'm doing okay?" "Will my teen do something to embarrass me and cause me to be disapproved of by others?" "Since society expects a parent to be caring and constantly responsible for teens, am I a bad parent if I begin to let go by not doing everything for my teen?" Parents asking themselves such questions need to work on their own lack of self-esteem (see Chapter Five).

People have compiled lists of what the good parent should do for his or her children. It is not realistic to make such lists. The needs of each child are different. What each child is willing to accept is different. Needs, and the ability to cooperate, change with time. For example, Tom did average work in school until the seventh grade. When Tom had trouble with his homework before the seventh grade, his parents helped him as needed. In the seventh grade Tom began to feel that his parents were too concerned about his grades. Tom's parents insisted on checking his homework every day when his grades fell. Tom felt he had no control over his life and resented his parents' interference. The more his parents tried to "help" with his homework, the less Tom studied. At a time when Tom was finally old enough to take responsibility for his schoolwork, his parents tried to become more controlling. Tom's schoolwork was his concern (a "his-life item" as defined in the book, *Step Teen*). A later chapter in this book will discuss how to determine the amount of difficulty your teen is having with cooperation and other issues. Another chapter will discuss how to deal with schools and other outside agencies.

FEAR OF NOT KNOWING WHAT TO DO WHEN NOT PARENTING

Many parents fear they will not know their place or role in life if they are not constantly parenting. Three children under ten years of age will keep a mother running. But when the children are all in their teens, constant attention is not always healthy or even appreciated. When their children start to grow up, some parents do not know what to do if they are not parenting. They may not know what or who they are or what their goal in life will be.

FEAR OF BEING UNABLE TO FUNCTION IN A CAREER

Some parents do not feel capable of doing anything but parenting; they have not functioned in school or the business world for years. On the other hand, parents who have been working may fear advancement or career changes. Both categories of parents may lack self-confidence, self-esteem, or belief in their powers of creativity. Without purpose, life can be empty. This fear is why many parents will not let go. Such parents must not only let go of their children's lives, they must also get hold of their own lives. These parents fear the uncertain challenges of new roles.

FEAR OF THE PAIN OF MOURNING LOSSES

Fear of experiencing painful feelings (such as mourning and sadness) when a child begins to separate may lead to destructive acting out by the parents. Rather than experience the hurt of separation, some parents may run from their feelings and engage in such destructive behavior as affairs and drinking. Acting on feelings, rather than experiencing them, is done in an attempt to avoid the inevitable painful feeling of separation. This is more likely to occur if the adult has had difficulty with other separations in the past. Separation, like letting go, is normally a gradual process which takes place in many small steps over the years.

We have a choice of how well we will respond to our teen's growing up. We can tighten our hold on our kids because of fear or a desire to avoid personal loss; or, our teens can remind us of our own dreams we had as teenagers. Our kids can stimulate us to revive our shelved possibilities and goals. Their growth can challenge us to pursue our own development. As an exercise, think about the factors listed in Table 2-4.

In Preparing to Let Go, Think About:
1. **Your adolescence**
2. **Separation from your parents**
3. **Your parents' style of child management**
4. **Your parents' losses when you were a teen**
5. **Your parents' fears when you were a teen**
6. **Your fears and losses as a teen**

Table 2-4.

Questions

These questions are meant to help you analyze your feelings and better understand how the material in this chapter applies to you. Whether or not your spouse has had time to read this book with you, discussing some of these questions with your spouse will help you work together on your problems so that you can treat your teen more consistently.

1. How did you feel about becoming more independent from your parents? Did you resent their involvement in your schoolwork, dates, curfew, choice of career or mate? How did you deal with these separation issues? How did your parents deal with these separation issues?

2. Did your parents give up vacations, career advancement, or time for their own enjoyment while you were taking their time and money for your own activities? How did you feel about this? How did they feel about their sacrifices? Were the sacrifices a mistake? Did you feel guilty and pressured to live up to parental expectations because of your parents' sacrifices?

3. Did you feel neglected and angry when your parents decreased the amount of responsibility they assumed for your life? How did you deal with this? How did they deal with it? Or, did your parents insist on maintaining or taking over more control in your life?

4. Did your parents make a career choice for you? Did they assume you would go to college or take a certain kind of job? How do you feel about that? Should you do this with your own children?

5. Do you now feel a loss of physical, sexual, or athletic abilities? Are these feelings of loss intensified by seeing these same qualities emerge in your teen?

6. Do you feel that caring for your teen has prevented or delayed your pursuing a career? Do you resent this? What do you plan to do about it?

7. Should you have the ability to make minute-by-minute decisions concerning your child's social, academic, drug-taking, smoking, athletic, sexual, and financial activities?

8. Assume the answer to the previous question is "Yes" at age seven and "No" at age nineteen. How can the teen gradually learn to make decisions on each of these topics? Remember that lectures may fall on deaf ears as the teenage years approach; learning comes through unbiased information and experience.

9. If you were not busy caring for your child, what would you do?

10. Do you consider it worth the time and money needed for you to take an exercise or night school course? If not, would you consider it worth the time and money if your child wanted to take such a course? If you think such things are worthwhile for your children, but not for you, explain why.

11. Does a trip to a museum or World's Fair mean more to you if the children come, even if they are not interested? Why?

12. Do you or your teen have plans for the teen's education and career? Do they coincide? Does the teen have a goal or drive in life? Do you?

13. Have you experienced feelings of normal or abnormal mourning due to changes in your child? Such feeling may include denial, sadness, anger, depression, and various degrees of acceptance of changes in your child. As the following chapters explain, you must have some of these feelings if you are to accept the fact that your child is becoming a separate person.

14. Do you fear the loss of your teen's love so much that you allow behavior you do not approve of?

15. What practical steps can you take concerning your fears for the physical safety of your teen? Do you actually have control over this?

3. Understanding Emotional Changes In Your Teenager

This is the painful part of growing:
Compassion for the child not yet its own
        — Kay Keeshan Hamod, poet

If this book is supposed to be about parental emotions, concerns, rights, and responsibilities, why— you ask— include a chapter on teenage emotions? This chapter aims to help parents understand, effectively react to, and accept their teen's age-appropriate behavior. Knowledge about and understanding of what is going on inside your teen's head can help you relate to his or her experiences and make more intelligent decisions in your relationship. Also, you will feel less hurt when you receive hostile or angry words from a teen if you realize the anger may have less to do with you than with the teen's own uncertainties. For example, a parent may feel guilty, rejected, or depressed when a teen argues about curfew and other rules. In this case the parent should understand that the teen may be looking for limits, testing his or her own new desire for more personal power, or generally seeing just how much he or she can get away with. Through these arguments teens can find out how secure, reliable, and confident parents are about their own beliefs and values. When a parent loosens discipline and allows rules to be changed on the basis of irrelevant arguments, ("Everyone is doing it"), the teen feels insecure and out of control. The nervousness and anger shown by the argumentative teen is often a sign of insecurity. Firmness (and fairness) help to bring calm and compliance from the teen in the long run.

41

The teen is most helped by the parent who works to reduce his or her own problems and conflicts. If the parent feels helplessness, depression, or anxiety, the teen senses this and becomes insecure, nervous about the future, and possibly quarrelsome. Family therapist and author J. Haley (*Ordeal Therapy*), discusses how building one mother's self-confidence was a major factor in helping a family deal with their very out-of-control younger children. These children constantly misbehaved and screamed. Rather than offering the mother child guidance management techniques or "training," the therapist working with this family focused on building the mother's self-confidence, talking about her future career plans, and strengthening the couple's marriage. The parents were given specific directives to show more affection to each other and to focus on their own common sense in managing their family. There was great improvement in the situation. These guidelines are also applicable to families with teens. The teen is trying to learn the rules of the environment; inconsistencies and uncertainties seem unfair and weak. A teen's tendency to argue may seem to indicate that the teen wants the parent to abdicate authority. However, this is usually not the case. It is age-appropriate for teens to want more power in decision-making, but an adolescent does not want total control from his parents. This would be frightening and upsetting for the adolescent. A gradual letting go of control over the teen, as the teen becomes more mature, is the goal.

Like anyone else, teens feel a sense of power when they accomplish something. Grades in school, repairing the car, athletic achievements, and musical ability will give the teen a sense of pride, self-confidence, and a genuine sense of social and personal effectiveness. A job can give a teen the sense of economic power. If the teen has gained a talent or an ability solely because of parental urging and pushing, the sense of accomplishment may be diluted, or even destroyed. The teen may feel the accomplishment is, to a great extent, due to the efforts of the parent. For example, one bright girl was barely passing work in school. Her parents hired tutors, bought her books, and coached her all they could. She continued to do poorly, taking very little interest in school. One day she asked her parents if they would pay for music lessons. They said they would not. The girl said, "You care so much about my education. Don't you care about my musical education?" The parents said, "If you choose to play an instrument, it is your financial responsibility." From that point on, the girl spent most of her free time playing the piano. She became extremely good at it, too.

Teens want to be independent, yet they are not capable of being totally autonomous. They know they want to learn how to be independent, but they also fear the responsibility that comes with growing up. Unasked-for guidance and advice are often met with hostility. The parent should not interpret hostility to parental control as rejection, but as a healthy sign that the teen wants to try to make some decisions without help. The most effective way to deal with a teen's behavioral, emotional, academic, or sports problems won't be found in the countless methods detailed in articles on these topics. The way to help is to view the adolescent and yourself as responsible, powerful individuals. For example, your teen says she would like to play tennis better. Instead of spending hours trying to teach her a proper tennis serve, it might be more effective to just say, "I know you will do well." You must feel enough self-confidence and power that you are willing to allow the teen to become responsible for his or her own desires, successes, and failures. You need to remind yourself that letting the teen make mistakes is appropriate parenting. Doing everything for the teen and therefore giving the illusion that the child is "perfect" is detrimental. You have to be strong enough to allow the teen to make and learn from mistakes (within reasonable limits). Attempt to radiate confidence in the teen, even when there are temporary setbacks. Showing a teen how to do everything can give the impression you believe the teen is helpless.

Coaching and "helping" will fail if you care more about the grades or sports than the teen. Emotional or physical problems of the teen will worsen if you stay up into the night with the "patient." Schoolwork won't be done consistently if you make yourself responsible for reminding the teen to do it.

Teens are skilled at sensing vulnerability and feelings of inferiority and helplessness in their parents. Consciously or subconsciously, teens may use parental sensitivities as a way to manipulate. Manipulation is hurtful for the teen as well as the parent. Any feelings of helplessness or inferiority you have felt for years may be responsible for your teen's habit of disregarding your wishes. For example, the teen may have seen over the years that you would be willing to bend just about any rule because you are vulnerable to religious pressure. The child has noted that there was no money for a new dress unless it was needed for church; bedtime was enforced unless there was a church activity that required attention; homework was not regularly monitored, but preparation for Confirmation was worried about, discussed, and monitored. A teen with this type of background might manipulate parents by refusing to attend services or asking for clothes because "everyone else at church" has a certain style of dress. Bending rules to encourage church participation has taught the teen that rules could be broken and given the teen experience in doing it.

Gaining self-respect and setting limits on your teen's behavior may initially provoke rage from your teen. Eventually the teen will gain feelings of security and stability when firm limits are set. Teens rebel but need (and subconsciously want) reasonable controls on their behavior. In the long run, people who manipulate do feel guilty about their behavior. Therefore, look upon setting limits on your teen as constructive parenting.

Identity Confusion

As we have seen, teens (as well as their parents) experience losses, challenges, and fear during adolescence. Teens experience loss and grief as they mature, although this may not seem the case to parents. Adolescence is a time for major biological, social, and cognitive changes. Although changes bring growth, they also bring loss.

Feelings of loss can lead to regressive behavior in adolescents. Such behavior can prevent parents from letting go by reinvolving them in issues that are more appropriately managed by the teen. For example Mary is a twelve-year-old girl. Her parents are asking her to assume more responsibility. She has just entered a junior high school that is five times as large as her grade school had been. Most of her former friends are going to different schools. Although Mary is excited about these changes, she feels a loss of friends, security, and a familiar routine. Mary does not know why she feels uneasy, but she does develop a significant amount of anxiety due to her losses. As a result, she acts surly, angry, and tense with her parents. It would help Mary's parents if they could understand why Mary is anxious...this does not imply that her parents should put up with the insulting or damaging behavior. However, knowing that Mary (like themselves) is experiencing loss during this transitional period might make it easier to be compassionate. This knowledge can help Mary's parents assist in dealing with the pressure in her life by encouraging her to meet new friends, or to seek counseling.

Another example of adolescent loss is that experienced by Joe. His father had left the family several times in the past, but has lived with them for the last four years. Though he drinks on weekends, Joe's father has stayed sober during the week and has supported the family during this time. Last week Joe's father got into a fight with his mother, broke her nose, and left home. Now Joe has been arrested for robbing a gas station. Though Joe should not be excused for his crime, it would help to understand that he might be reacting to the belief that he has lost his father, a good part of the family income, and a bit of his family stability. Joe has experienced a significant loss and is unsure of his role. Is he now the "man of the house?" He may be asking himself basic questions such as "Who am I?" and "Where am I?" Besides the loss of his father, Joe feels that he has abruptly lost his childhood.

PEER PRESSURES

Relationships with peers and other people become important in the teen years. Dress, hair styles, and behavior often change to impress peers rather than parents. Most adults can remember using cigarettes, alcohol, and foul language at various times in their teen years in an effort to "fit in." Now that alcohol and other drugs are more readily available, efforts to please peers and experimentation can have long-lasting and serious consequences.

MATURATION

Kids' feelings and ways of thinking change at this age; as a result, their behavior changes. Let's look at some of the major emotional and mental developmental changes teens undergo, and the concomitant behavioral changes that occur because of these growth surges.

Loss of:
1. Security of childhood   4. Perfect parents
2. Freedom from responsibility 5. Security
3. Identity

Table 3-1. Losses Teens Often Feel

LOSS OF SECURITY

During adolescence, children lose their illusions regarding the nature of family life. Security, permanence, and stability are lessened by growth and independence. Although children want to move towards independence, another part of them wants to hold on to the security and lack of responsibility of childhood. These emotions regarding loss are often unconsciously felt, yet the feelings do exist and influence children's behavior. With increasing biological and intellectual growth, the young teen is challenged by increasing social and academic responsibilities. Assuming increasing responsibility and decision-making gives an individual a sense of independence. However, independence can also bring fears, uneasiness, insecurity, and a sense of one's essential aloneness in the universe. In order to become adults, teens must give up some of their attachment to, and dependence on, parents. This need for, and yet fear of, increasing independence is one reason that the adolescent's peer group becomes so important.

The peer group helps to decrease those feelings of insecurity and aloneness as the teen moves away from total dependence on family. The peer group acts as a transitional bridge between total dependence on parents and family structure in childhood and the move towards individuation and responsibility of adulthood.

LOSS OF FREEDOM FROM RESPONSIBILITY

The young teen is an expert at being a child and a total novice at being a responsible adult. Although the growing teen gains much, the decrease in dependence and security of childhood is a major loss for the teen. Teens naturally want independence and privileges. However, responsibility and accountability often accompany the independence or privileges teens desire. This can cause much anxiety. For example, John wants to be able to drive the family car on Saturday nights. He becomes responsible and accountable for following traffic rules and not driving while drunk. John knows that if he gets drunk or stoned on drugs and injures someone while driving, he is in some sense responsible for the injuries. This moral responsibility remains, even if John's father gets a lawyer to fix the legal problems associated with the "accident." The existence of responsibility and accountability which go beyond flexible parental demands is a valid reason for anxiety in teens. Most teens are able to face the responsibilities associated with driving, moving away from home eventually, and assuming new roles in life.

LOSS OF IDENTITY

Changes in the way a teen thinks lead to a change in self-image. Although teens work at establishing a new self-image for several years, the loss of identity associated with being a child is still felt. As a child becomes a teenager, there is a loss of the sense of being the center of the universe. Young children see the world as revolving around them. They tend to be very egocentric and think that they have much more control over events than they actually do. They see their wishes and feelings as having great power. Younger children also tend to believe that other people must think and feel what they are thinking and feeling. The process of growth is a process of moving from a preoccupation with the self to a greater capacity for relativistic thinking and empathy for others' feelings. The growing child begins to see that he has very limited control and power over events and that other people have different viewpoints than he does. These changes in perspective are deflating to the teen. Some teens counter feelings of decreasing power and control by imagining the grandiose Utopian world they will create. Some teens escalate childhood manipulations when they are fearful of losing power and control. For example, some teens convincingly argue that it is impossible for them to get up ten minutes earlier in the morning before school in order not to leave the kitchen a mess...after all, five hours a day in school plus homework is a hard schedule. The teens expect their parents to clean up after them, even if their parents are working full-time. Over time, experience will hopefully intervene and bring the teen's expectations more in line with reality.

Meanwhile, however, teens may experience depression over the recognition that the school system, for instance, will not rescue them like mother always did, and the world will not change at their wish. Their thinking does not hold the power they have always felt it had. Parental expectations are changing. The teen may be surprised to see that others have feelings that they want taken seriously.

The teen may eventually realize that there are straight and nonstraight ways of getting power. Taking responsible actions, such as driving safely and helping pay car expenses, would be an example of a straight way to get power. Arguing that everyone gets the use of the family car and refusing to do chores around the house would be a non-straight, or manipulative way of getting power.

In line with these changes, the teen may find himself experiencing a loss of identity. The teen's parents may also be unsure of their roles at work and at home. During early adolescence, as the teen views himself and his parents, there is a change in how the teen views himself and his parents. The teen emotionally and intellectually begins a process of identifying with or discarding various aspects of the parents' (and other significant figures') personalities. It is almost as if the childhood personality loosens up, rearranges itself, and incorporates aspects of adult personality modes (especially parents) that will ultimately allow the teen to fill future roles that used to be filled by parents. Aspects of the identities of significant others which are meaningful to the teen will be incorporated into the teen's newly reorganizing sense of self. Although the teen is growing, there may be a sense of identity diffusion that results in confusion — a not knowing "who I am anymore" — until the more mature personality solidifies. In the meantime, the teen may try out several new identities. The old self is changing, yes, but there must be loss before there can be growth. Before a toddler walks he reverts back to crawling to gain confidence, and then he advances.

LOSS OF PERFECT PARENTS

A young child will idealize his or her parents and not see their faults. As the child gets older, thinking ability increases. The older child questions, compares, and remembers better than the younger child. At the same time the child notes vulnerabilities and sensitivities of the parents. By the time the child is ten or twelve years old, the parents' lack of consistent discipline, inability to do everything the "ideal" or "good" parent should, and other imperfections are noted by the child. Some children become very angry when they realize that their childhood image of their parents has been inaccurate. They may feel cheated when they identify real or imagined defects in their parents. Bringing these imperfections to the attention of the parents may result in guilt feelings. If recognition of these parental imperfections results in the child feeling cheated, he or she may take on the role of a victim. The child may feel that other parents spend more time and money on their children. The victim role may be strengthened when the child notes that promises made by his or her parents are not always kept. The result is a hurt, revengeful child and self-blaming, guilt-ridden parents.

The teen may mourn for all the losses mentioned above. This process of mourning will be discussed further in later chapters.

ADOLESCENTS' FEARS ASSOCIATED WITH LETTING GO

The threat of losses listed above may cause the emotional response of fear. Fears of the adolescent are listed in the table below.

Fear of:
1. Losses and the pain of mourning
2. The unknown (changed individuals and family)
3. Physical dangers
4. Contradicting expectations of peer group
5. Not having a well-defined role in life, especially if not constantly directed
6. Loss of love
7. Roles: occupational, sexual, and social
8. Physical attractiveness, or lack of it
9. Changes in lifestyle
10. Decreasing sense of power

Table 3-2. Teenagers' Fears Associated With Letting Go

The adolescent takes a new leap in intellectual abilities when he or she begins to enter a new cognitive stage called formal operation. Up to now, the child was very specific and concrete in his or her thinking. In the teen years, the new thinking ability to abstract and draw general conclusions allows the teen to work with English literature and algebra in school and to recognize inconsistencies and vulnerabilities in parents at home. As stated by Paul Henry Mussen in *Child Development and Personality* (Mussen, Conger, and Kagan), "In contrast to the child who is preoccupied, for the most part, with learning how to function in the world of 'here and now,' the adolescent is able 'not only to grasp the immediate state of things but also the possible state they might or could assume.' For example, the adolescent's new-found and frequently wearing talents for discovering his previously idealized parents' feet of clay — for questioning their values, comparing them with other, 'more understanding' or 'less square' parents, accusing them of 'hypocritical' inconsistencies between professed values and behavior — all appear at least partly dependent on the adolescent's changes in cognitive ability. The awareness of the discrepancy between the actual and the possible also helps to make the adolescent a rebel. He is always comparing the possible with the actual and discovering that the actual is frequently 'wanting'...A good deal of an adolescent's apparently passionate concern with the deficiencies of parents and the social order and with the creation of 'viable alternatives' often turns out to be primarily verbal, more a matter of work than deed. This is perhaps a reflection of the fact that this stage of cognitive development is still relatively new and not yet fully integrated into the adolescent's total adaptation to life."

With the beginning of formal mental operations, the teen begins to acquire the ability to abstract and hypothesize about the world. The teen can now speculate on the future and his place in the world. Thinking about future occupational, sexual, and social roles is a new preoccupation of the teen. Prior to this time, the child was quite concrete and did not think much beyond the immediate situation.

Thinking ahead can be frightening to the teen. "What will I do in the future?" "Am I smart enough to make college or get the job I want?" "Will I be gay?" "Will anyone marry me?" "Do I really believe in the religion or morality to which my parents ascribe?" These kinds of thoughts resulting from this new ability to speculate and weigh possibilities can be quite frightening to the teen. Again, new abilities arouse insecurities. It is this new capacity for abstract thinking that contributes to teens' insecurities about themselves, as well as criticism of their parents.

Fears, especially fear of loss of the parent's love, may make the teen hold on tighter to the parent rather than become more independent. Some parents, especially those who are somewhat depressed, may for many years inadvertently send the message to their teen that if the teen grows up and away, the parent will become quite depressed. The teen may feel that to grow up would hurt his parent and cause that parent actual pain. Without actually being aware of this kind of behavior, some parents may look and sound very depressed every time the teen makes an independent move toward adulthood. Such parents are often not feeling support from any relationship other than that with their child. The child may get the feeling that he or she is required to make the parent feel better. Such a teen may feel very guilty about establishing new relationships outside the parent-teen orbit. Children of depressed parents are often very sensitive to any indication that they are upsetting their parents. They may feel guilty about a slight look of sadness around the parent's mouth or a soft sigh when the teen announces that she is thinking of attending college away from home. If you are depressed, it is extremely important that you seek help for yourself and don't attempt to use your teen to make you feel better. Remember, this stage of life requires grieving for both parent and child. Don't use your child to assuage your depression and grief. It will not work and will cause problems for your teen as well.

Parents with other problems, especially alcoholism, also need professional help. Seeking help to improve one's situation is not an admission of failure or guilt.

Up to now, we have discussed some of the less tangible fears and uncertainties experienced by teens. However, there are many practical concerns of living that may also upset the teen during this time. The need to eventually assume the role of breadwinner, homemaker, and parent is often a worry to the teen. Teens may be apprehensive about the job market, getting into college, or being attractive to the opposite sex so that they can find a spouse. This is a time when private worries and practical fears can merge into a chronic state of concern for the teen.

Adolescents' Ways of Dealing With Fear

Child psychologist Dan Kiley (*Keeping Kids Out of Trouble*), describes how teens' use of tough, detached attitudes is often a cover for the fear and insecurity which can result for a poorly defined identity. Kids who convey the following attitude to their parents and teachers are often quite scared underneath their bravado exterior:

You can't hurt me, 'cause I don't care.
You punish me here, I'll go there.
You have your rules, that's good to see,
But what you don't understand
Is that it don't mean nothin' to me.

Parents, according to Kiley, who take this coolness and detachment as rejection are misinterpreting the teens' meaning. "It" does not refer to punishment or the parental/teacher authority. Rather, "it" refers to the kid's identity or soul. When young teens begin to lose their childhood identity, they get scared. Instead of becoming panicky or depressed about how bad they feel, they depersonalize their "self." They call this new feeling of emptiness within themselves "it." Thus, the real lyrics of the song are "I don't mean nothing to me."

It takes a two-pronged approach to deal with a teen who is experiencing these feelings. On one hand, the teen needs to be held accountable for all responsibilities and transgressions. On the other hand, poor self-concept and painful feelings of emptiness can be eased by having someone to talk with about the kid's search for meaning and new importance. If the song continues unchanged for too long, the teen's identity formation is delayed. The "It don't mean nothing to me" kid may sit on the sidelines, afraid to engage constructively in life. Eventually, this type of kid will probably fail to develop a strong sense of self, or he may act in antisocial and destructive ways.

Emotionally distancing yourself or bribing your teen are inappropriate and unhealthy means of avoiding the pain due to loss and change. We will talk later about how parents can react constructively to changes in teens' emotional behavior. However, it is important to realize that much adolescent behavior that we may be labeling "indifference" or rejection by your children is really age-appropriate and positive. For example, teens may begin to confide in peers instead of family, spend less time in family activities, and appear to reject many parental values. As Kolodny, Bratter, and Deep say in *How to Survive Your Adolescent's Adolescence,* "...it is vitally important for teenagers to begin to see their parents as real human beings, with shortcomings and imperfections, rather than as the omniscient parent figures seen by younger children. During this time, teenagers may criticize their parents or reject many of their values, not out of disrespect as much as a sign of growth and maturation." It is important that the parent realize that the teen is trying to find his or her own identity. The teen is not deliberately rejecting the parent. If the parent can realize this, there is less chance of emotionally withdrawing in anger or attempting to win back the love of the little one by being overly solicitous of the child.

However, if a teen attempts to define himself by embracing antisocial values and behavior, then the parent will need to set firm and consistent consequences. This may also mean involving a law enforcement agency or joining a parent support group to speak with parents having similar concerns. Counseling for parent and adolescent may also be in order.

Teens' Unrealistic Expectations

Teenagers, as well as some adults, often have the unrealistic expectation that life should be fair. Parents are pressured to give late curfews, large allowances, and other favors because "other parents do it," or "everybody gets it." You, as a parent, must make up your own mind about what is within your means and what will disrupt your life. Perhaps many other parents do watch their kid's sports events, but you are working sixty hours a week. Besides, the teen must eventually learn to enjoy activities without your constant interest and supervision. Teens do continue to need a certain amount of quality time with their parents, but they can function on their own much of the time.

The teen may have real problems, concerns, and pressures. The teen may feel you have not been the best parent. Perhaps you have been inconsistent with discipline, short on money, divorced several times, or even drunk at times. Still, this does not give the teen the right to make your life difficult. Nor does it give you the responsibility of sacrificing more than you are comfortable with of your own time, life, and resources to please your teen. A reasonable course of action is to admit your mistakes, change your behavior, and hold your teen accountable for what he or she does.

Summary

Parents will have less guilt and anxiety if they realize that they are not responsible for their teen's undesirable behavior. Teens often act in what appears to be an irrational manner because they are feeling losses and fears. To cope with loss and fear, teens test limits set by their parents and the rest of the world. When a parent holds firm to a limit, the teen actually feels more secure. Teens also have behavioral problems because they are hoping to gain power, escape the pain of growth, and define new identities. Teens are losing the security and carefreeness of childhood and facing the fears associated with being an adult.

Understanding these reasons for teenage behavior can help parents react to them with compassion and firmness instead of hurt and anger.

4 Accepting Your Teen's Growth

In dealing with children
the left hand should push them away and
the right hand should draw them near.
— *Rabbi Shimon ben Elazar,*
discussing the Talmud

The previous chapters have described the various losses adolescence can bring for both teens and their parents. When there is a loss, a mourning reaction occurs. The purpose of mourning and grieving is to help an individual deal with the loss. Through mourning one gives up someone or something that has been meaningful and important. One learns to accept the loss, and when grieving is completed, the individual begins to feel a stronger sense of self.

The following chapters will advise you how to fashion your life by focusing on your self-confidence, self-respect, and life goals. You might not be getting along with your teen or your teen may be in trouble with the law. The following chapters will help you to

Mourn your losses
Face your fears
Find meaning in your own life
Define your identity
Make new commitments

Table 4-1. Steps Needed to Prepare Yourself for Growth

develop your self, even if there is a lack of cooperation from your teen, the schools, and the courts.

Before you can build your own life, however, you must accept the fact that your "little baby" is now a separate person. Your teen is an independent being separate from you and not entirely under your control.

Grief and Mourning

To accept the losses discussed in previous chapters, you must go through the stages of mourning which are commonly associated with accepting the death of a loved one. In reality, the young child you used to care for is gone. A teenager is there now.

When areas crucial to self-definition and a sense of life's meaning have been lost, there is a normal grief reaction: grief is a common universal reaction to loss. Many scholars have studied the grief reaction, and have determined that there are certain sequential stages that occur during grief. What are these stages and how do they apply to the child-parent relationship during the adolescent years?

---

1. Denial and the impulse to remain attached; the protest stage of separation (anger)
2. Intellectual acceptance of separation
3. Emotional acceptance of separation
4. Detachment and new identification
5. Formation of adult-adult interactions with teen

Table 4-2. The Stages of Mourning

In his book, *Adolescent-Parental Separation*, Michael V. Bloom compares parent/child separation to the process of bereavement. Although there are obvious differences (i.e., there is not a complete ending to the relationship), the "powerful young child-to-parent relationship so necessary to earlier child development must now die in order to allow the young adult to pursue independently his or her future," writes Bloom. The former way of relating must be replaced by a new parent-to-young adult relationship. According to Bloom, "In order to make this change, many needs that were previously fulfilled by the relationship must be withdrawn before other modes of relating can be established. In essence, certain expectations, modes of response, and fulfillments must die."

The Stages of Mourning

DENIAL

Stage One of Mourning.
Denial and the Impulse to Remain Attached: the Protest
Threat of the loss of a significant person in our lives may activate panic. We may experience the feeling of not knowing who we are. These frightening and painful feelings may cause denial of the loss and there may be frantic attempts to reattach with the lost person. This may be a loss due to death or the threatened break-up of a close relationship. Since both parent and young teen are experiencing loss, there is a natural tendency for both to want to deny the pain of loss and remain attached. Thus, "the motivation for separation is highly ambivalent" (Bloom). Control is needed over those parts of both parents and adolescents that compel them to remain attached. This is particularly difficult to do because both parent and child feel a sense of lost identity and want to hold on to the familiar. An image that can be associated with this stage is that of the adolescent and parent holding onto each other with one hand, while pushing as hard as possible with the other (Bloom). The pushing-away image symbolizes the parent's desire to see the child grow and the teen's desire to develop independence. The holding-on of parent and child in this scene illustrates the conflicting impulse to stay attached. Fear of the impending separation and attempts to deny and prevent the loss are basic to the first stage of grief. Behaviorally, this stage of grief may manifest itself in constant parent-teen conflicts.

Both parent and teen may feel the early stages of separation occurring and may hold on to each other through constant fighting. The parent, wishing to be needed, may continually get involved in the teen's life items. A teen's life items are those problems which involve the teen alone that are usually best solved by him or her alone. Examples of a teen's life items include appearance, hygiene, school grades, and neatness of the teen's room. The teen's room does not affect anyone else (unless there is a smell or it attracts insects). The neatness of the family bathroom may affect others and is, therefore, not a teen's life item. If a teen asks for help or advice with any of his or her life items, the parent can feel free to give advice.

However, advice not asked for often leads to useless arguing. This is especially true when the advice is given repeatedly. The teen begins to resent unnecessary supervision and the parents become frustrated in their attempts to gain control; a power struggle usually is the result. Thus, bickering may appear to be a sign of separation, but it is really an indication that parent and teen are caught in Stage One (denial).

However, if the parent begins to offer the teen more responsibility, the teen may purposely fail, thus inviting the parent to take control. This way the teen avoids the fear that accompanies the act of assuming increased responsibility. Just like the image described above, there is pushing and pulling at the same time (as evidenced by increasing numbers of power struggles), but no real separation. Both parent and teen are stuck in the stage of anger and blaming. By blaming each other, the parent and teen avoid responsibility for their own decisions and lives. This early stage of mourning and separation, although painful and confusing for both parent and child, is preferable to the situation where there are no attempts at separation. In this situation, as the parent and child get older, future attempts to separate become more difficult and abnormal. Separation normally occurs gradually, involving more and more aspects of the teen's life as the years go by.

For example, Sue suffered from itching and other allergic reactions to milk products. Avoiding milk products was difficult because they are put into so many prepared foods. When Sue was nine years old, an allergist prescribed monthly allergy shots to decrease Sue's reactions. The shots seemed to help. When Sue was eleven, her mother stopped taking time off work to drive her to the clinic because she felt Sue was old enough to take the bus to get her shots. Sue's mother always reminded her to go for her allergy shots and thought she was getting them. One day Sue's mother happened to be off work and gave Sue a ride there. The clinic called later to say that Sue had been treated for a serious reaction to her allergy shot. Sue had failed to tell the nurse that she had missed several shots, a factor important in determining how strong a dosage should be given. Sue's parents expressed their surprise at Sue's missing her injections. Sue said she did not think it was worthwhile to spend two hours catching buses to and from the clinic; she did not believe the shots were helpful and refused to go unless she was driven. Sue was sure she was "growing out" of her allergies.

Sue's mother decided not to drive Sue to get the shots. She also decided not to sit up with Sue at night when itching kept her awake. Sue was allowed to make a decision for herself. If the decision did not work out, Sue would be allowed to decide to resume the shots. Her mother felt that Sue might learn a lesson which would influence Sue's future thinking about other health issues, including sex and birth control.

On the other hand, eighteen-year-old Ralph was getting an ulcer from drinking beer. His parents did not consider the drinking to be simply a "his-life item." The problem also belonged to his parents because Ralph's behavior, when he was drinking, disrupted the entire family. Ralph was sent to the local Detox Center every time he came home drunk. Seeing the older chronic alcoholics at the Detox Center did more to curb Ralph's drinking than years of lectures from his parents.

When Stage One is successfully accomplished, the impulse to remain attached is controlled. When the parent and teen are motivated to grow, the next stage of mourning and separation begins. Successful completion of Stage One occurs gradually over time and is signaled by the ability of the parents to give up trying to control the teen's life items such as school grades, non-fatal health issues, dress, neatness of the teen's room, hours the teen keeps (within the legal curfew and local safety conditions), and friends the teen makes. At the same time, the teen is allowed to make decisions in these areas. The decisions need not be correct, and the parents will not interfere, unless the decisions invade the parent's life space.

For example, if the teen decides to associate with drug users, the parents may find they cannot stop the teen. Their teen may, in fact, be trying to get his friend off drugs. If, however, their teen starts to use drugs and subjects the parents to unreasonable behavior, the drug abuse becomes a parental problem. This takes the situation out of the "teen's-life item" category.

INTELLECTUAL ACCEPTANCE

Stage Two of Mourning.
The Easing of Denial and Protest:
An Intellectual Acceptance of Separation
As the inevitability of change and development becomes apparent to teen and parent, an intellectual awareness of change is demonstrated. For the teen, this cognitive acceptance of change

may be demonstrated by taking on a part-time job to show increasing financial independence. There may be greater physical distance between parent and child. This distancing may be noticed by a decreasing number of family outings, the teen's spending a great deal of time away from home or in his room, and a decrease in conversation between parent and teen. The parent may also be expecting more adult-like behavior from the early teen in many areas. The teen may make a point of espousing belief systems that differ from parental values, just to prove to self and parent that separation is starting to occur. Similar to the grief reaction over a death, there may be intellectual understanding of separation prior to actual emotional acceptance of separation.

EMOTIONAL ACCEPTANCE OF SEPARATION

Stage Three of Mourning.
The Emotional Stage of Grieving

Up to this point, there has been a denial of the separation at the feeling level. Although both parent and teen intellectually understand that changes are occurring, they may try to deny the painful feelings of loss by "holding-on behaviors" (i.e., power struggles, irresponsibility on the part of the teen, and oversolicitousness of the part of the parent). Both parent and teen may unconsciously collude at staying angry at each other so they will not have to experience the painful feelings of loss that typify this stage. This is evidenced when both parties begin to pick fights with each other as a way of avoiding sadness. Anger is easier to tolerate than the sadness of mourning. The third stage of the normal mourning process cuts through denial on the part of the parent and teen, and both begin to experience the pain and depression of separation. This is the stage that is most characterized by feelings of depression and sometimes despair. Both parties' sadness at their loss is truly experienced. There may be feelings of rejection as the child develops values different from the parents'.

For example, Delbert's parents came from families in which every child became a doctor, lawyer, accountant, or successful professional of some sort. Delbert's parents were both professors at a university. When Delbert's high school grades fell, his parents tried monitoring his homework, hiring tutors, sending him to special classes, and forcing him to go to summer school. Delbert, however, kept a C average and spent all the time he could playing football. His grades never did come up, but he did get into college with a football scholarship. He did quite well once he was away from his parents; emotional acceptance never came until Delbert obtained his scholarship. The painful years of attempting to control Delbert were wasted.

Until this stage of mourning is successfully completed, it may be characterized by depression. Both parent and teen may also experience anger and guilt during this time. Neither party wants to feel sadness. Therefore, both may be angry at having to experience sadness and loss. Many people feel that it is wrong to feel anger, so they begin to feel guilty. Thus, on top of sadness during this stage of mourning, there can also be layers of anger and guilt. As described above, rather than experiencing these, parents and teens may act out painful emotions through rebellion, constant fighting, and psychological symptomatology.

Most parents want their children to grow up, but part of a parent may also be frightened about what this change will mean in terms of the parent's life. Thus, coupled with sadness, the parent may also experience anger and fear regarding the change in family life. Additionally, the parent may feel anger over having to tolerate the upsetting feelings of sadness. With successful mourning, parents may feel relief rather than fear.

In cases where the parent feels guilty about his anger, perhaps the parent is thinking, "I shouldn't have these feelings of sadness about my kid growing up. The fact that I am feeling sad means that there is something wrong with me. Maybe I am selfish. What's worse, sometimes I am even angry at my child for having newfound independence. I'm guilty over my anger and sadness." The parent who feels guilty at this stage may deny any anger or sadness. This denial complicates the mourning process. Reaching the final stage of mourning may also be made more difficult if the teen is exhibiting extremely disruptive behavior. This may cause the parents to become stuck in the anger stage, thus making separation even more difficult.

Similarly, the young teen is experiencing strong conflicting emotions about the sadness of separation. Besides dealing with his own uncertainty and fears, the teen may sense the parent's pain over this stage and deduce that his growth is damaging the parent. This stage of mourning can be exceptionally difficult for the parent or teen who does not have a strong sense of self. A parent with a weak sense of self may be chronically depressed or very controlling. Teens of depressed or controlling parents can be especially vulnerable to separation difficulties. They may feel that they are hurting their depressed parents even more with their normal growth. The adolescent's development of psychological symptoms (such as bulimia, anorexia, excessive fears, or depression) is often the teen's mistaken way of protecting the parent from the teen's independence. Rather than grow up and hurt the parent, the teen will stay small and sacrifice independence. Similarly, teens of very controlling parents (who are often depressed) may feel that they have to go along with the parent's control or lose that parent's love. Because of the parents' own feelings of inadequacy, they may try to be perfect parents and raise perfect children. If a teen does not fit the parents' view of the perfect adolescent, the parents may exert more control. Such parents see their children as an extension of themselves rather than as separate individuals. The teen frequently perceives an emotional withdrawal from a depressed, controlling parent whenever the teen makes an independent step toward growth. Such parents are often in deep emotional pain themselves and are not aware of how their depression and need for control may be affecting their children. Their own chronic "neediness" is exacerbated during this period of parental loss (adolescence).

The teen may then begin to experience anger at the parent for making him or her feel guilty about becoming independent. The teen may get stuck in this anger stage of separation (constantly engaging in rebellious behavior as a result) and never really experience the grieving that comes with growing up and moving away from childhood. By behaving in ways which cause problems, the teen keeps the parent occupied and avoids the responsibilities that come with mature behavior. Both parent and teen stay angry and connected.

Psychological symptoms (such as fears, binge eating, depression, or starvation) can denote anger at the parent for supposedly making the teen feel guilty about independence as well as make a statement about the teen's attempt for independence (e.g., "You can't make me eat!" says the anorexic). These symptoms also serve to keep the parent tied to the teen, for some parents are easily manipulated by the excessive fears (phobias) or compulsive behaviors associated with the teenage years. A parent who gives into these fears by preparing food in a certain way demanded by the teen would support the teen's abnormal behavior and delay separation in an unhealthy manner. These symptoms serve multiple purposes. They keep the fearful teen dependent. They protect the teen and parent from normal grief. And, they allow the teen to express a quiet, manipulative anger at the parents. Instead of responsible, respected independent management of the teen's life items by the teen, an upsetting, nonproductive situation exists, such as when a parent continuously worries about what a teen eats.

Fortunately, most families do not experience such extreme difficulties during a teen's adolescence. However, most families do spend a good deal of time in an anger stage (arguing, rebellious behavior, and the like) before moving on to the experience of grief and detachment.

A NEW SELF-IMAGE

Stage Four of Mourning.
Detachment and New Identification

In this stage the adolescent begins to feel responsible and secure as a person who is separate from his or her parents. Decisions are made independently of the parents, though a son or daughter sometimes identifies with the parent whose values have earlier been rejected. For example, the parents' religious beliefs, career decisions, or methods of parenting may be adopted with some modification after years of "rejecting the parent's values," although only those values that are also meaningful to the adolescent tend to be adopted (Bloom).

The teen must form a new identity and discover new meaning in adult tasks before making the transition from childhood to adulthood. Similarly, the parent may need to find a new identity and meaning in life before it is possible to LET GO. In this new identification stage it can be helpful for parents to recognize the loss of satisfaction which has come with separation of the teen and to find other, possibly similar satisfactions without the teen. For example, if a parent enjoyed playing tennis with the children, the parent might continue to play tennis when the children are gone. In this stage the parents can benefit from the teen's separation by taking pride in the teen's successful independent existence, taking it as a sign of successful parenting (Bloom).

As the parent of a young child, most of your time and the meaning of your life may have been tied up with your child. As your son or daughter enters the teen years, you must let go of the old meaning of your life — the child. You must find new meaning in other areas of your life such as religion, social activities, or a career. Replace being a parent of a young adult with personal productivity, nature, religion, creativity, and new commitments.

New commitments can give you a new identification. You may help others, learn, or improve your health. As you will see later, you can find new meaning in life through pursuing a career, doing community work, or engaging in other rewarding activities. Incompleteness, despair, and the need to be busy as a "parent" in order to be fulfilled are put aside. The chances of anxiety and depression are lessened as the teen is accepted for what he or she is and as the parent develops new activities and interests.

As parents lose the need to devote themselves to the tasks of parenting younger children, they sometimes find their lives devoid of purpose and meaning. Their spiritual and religious goals in life may have been to raise "fine" children. The parents' social contacts and activities may have centered around sports and other activities of the children. The parents may have only felt they were doing what they "should" in life when they were attending to the needs of their children. When children no longer need constant nurturing, parents may feel spiritual and social emptiness. After successfully mourning for the losses associated with the children maturing, the parents may discover a need to expand their own identities and purposes in life. Chapter Five tells how to do this.

NEW RELATIONSHIPS

Stage Five of Mourning.
Mature Relationships

The child and parent finally end up with new values and life goals. As their relationship changes over the years, they get over the grief associated with the loss of the parent-child relationship. At this stage, parent and adolescent begin to develop an adult-to-adult relationship which is not based on control or dependency. Parents and teens come to feel like secure, separate individuals.

Guilt is sometimes derived from thoughts about "the debt owed to your parents for years of child-raising" or "the mistakes you made raising me." When mature relationships are established, such guilt is put aside. It is recognized that everyone makes mistakes.

The final interactions are adult-adult in nature, and the parent and adolescent become responsible for themselves (Bloom). Many parents and their grown children never do reach this stage.

5 Ways of Fortifying Yourself

You, the parent, must strengthen yourself if you are to successfully mourn the losses and face the fears described in previous chapters. You must strengthen yourself if you are going to allow your teen to mature, by letting go of concerns which are really your teen's personal business. It is very difficult to let go if you do not have a strong, secure sense of yourself. If you are to go through the stages of mourning described in the last chapter, you will need continued inspiration and fortification.

Fortifying Yourself Will Facilitate the Mourning Process

Techniques for dealing with each stage in the mourning process are given in this chapter. Even people who thoroughly understand these stages sometimes have difficulty working through them. Try to understand how the stages are relevant to you and your teen. You may be in different stages with various issues. For example, you may allow your teen to be responsible and independent when it comes to schoolwork, yet try to retain control over the teen's choice of friends.

As stated earlier, Stage One of mourning is characterized by denial and the impulse to remain attached. In this first stage of mourning the parent and child both realize the loss of their old ways of relating; there is an uncertainty of identity. Parent and child are both confused about who they are and what their roles should be. Stage Two of mourning involves the parent's and teen's intellectual acceptance of separation. Stage Three of mourning involves their emotional acceptance of separation. Stage Four of mourning, detachment, and new identification is a continuation of the previous stages. Stage Five of mourning, the development of mature relationships, permits both the teen and the parent to grow, develop personal strengths, and choose interests to pursue in life. The parent and child then feel adequately secure to separate and relate in an adult-to-adult way.

Techniques for Dealing With Stage One

In Stage One there is denial and the impulse to remain attached. Techniques which are helpful in this stage are ones that get you to confront the denial that separation is occurring, strengthen yourself, keep your self respect, and be objective about your teen's behavior. The pain of acknowledging that the child is growing away from you can be lessened when you begin to feel a more secure and stronger sense of self.

CONFRONTING DENIAL

The best confronter of a parent's natural tendency to want to hold on to a youngster is the teen's own physical, intellectual, and emotional growth. Some parents may find it very useful to look closely at and listen carefully to their developing adolescent. It is hard to deny that a son or daughter who is taller than the parent and is dating steadily is still a child. You may want to remind yourself that your teen is physically and intellectually almost an adult whenever you feel a pull to return to treating him or her like a child. Take a good look at the size of your "child."

The hardest time to confront denial is when the teen continues to act immaturely. Adolescents may exhibit childish behaviors that range from simple selfishness or absentmindedness (e.g., tying up the phone for hours) to infantile but destructive temper tantrums (e.g., pounding on walls). At these times, you may tell yourself that your teen is "still a kid," or "all teens do this," and therefore deny that the teen is capable of more mature behavior. This is a parental avoidance manuever which denies the teen's growth and capabilities. Parents often deny that a teen is a separate individual, growing away from parental control. This is an especially important time to confront denial regarding a child's emerging adulthood.

By confronting your tendency to deny your teen's growth and capabilities, you also strengthen yourself. You are defining the limits of behavior that you can tolerate. When you take action to see that you are not abused, you are telling yourself that you have rights worth defending. Taking self-protective action will not only strengthen your sense of self; it will also help your teen to mature. Through your actions, the teen learns what behaviors others are willing to tolerate. Like an athlete who develops a stronger body with constant practice, the parent and teen will both experience a stronger sense of self when parents realistically work to view their teens as young adults instead of big kids.

Mary's parents did deny her abilities and therefore suffered abuse for several years. Mary borrowed her mother's clothes, often keeping certain items for months at a time and sometimes staining or tearing expensive dresses. Mary also tied up the telephone for hours. Her parents believed she was just too young to care for clothes properly and too "immature" to use the telephone reasonably. When Mary was sixteen, her mother was upset by how few clothes she had in good condition, and Mary's father was upset about missing business calls. Mary's mother reclaimed her borrowed clothes. A time limit was put on telephone calls. When Mary ignored the time limit, she lost the use of the telephone. Through these actions Mary's parents gained self-respect, not to mention clothes and the use of their telephone. Mary began to learn to respect the property of others and gained experience in practicing self-control and responsibility.

CONFRONTING DENIAL BY REMEMBERING

To help confront your denial of the teen's development, keep a list of the teen's upsetting behaviors. Some parents need to get mad before they can see a situation realistically. Examples of such a list might be:

2/2/86 Dented the car while parking. Not only refused to help pay for the damages, but said it was my fault because the windows were not clean.

2/6/86 English teacher called to say he was disrupting the class. He swore at the teacher and also at me when I tried to discuss his classroom behavior.

2/10/86 Twenty dollars missing from my wallet. He denies knowing about it, but bought a new record album after being "flat broke" the day before.

2/13/86 Charged $176.00 worth of new clothes on my credit card. He may have needed some of the clothes, but certain items were overpriced. He refuses to return them.

The list may generate anger, but the list and your anger will not be useful if they cause you just to criticize or lecture the teen. Rather, use the list to help you define what actions you must take to enhance your own sense of worth and self-respect. Also, use the list to determine what behaviors will be tolerated and what limits must be set. Use your anger to make you determined to stick to the limits you set. For example, a parent reviewing the above list might decide to hide money, credit cards, and car keys. The parent might also decide not to respond when spoken to with foul language. If the teen responded with appropriate behavior for a week, the parent might consider returning driving privileges on a trial basis when the car repairs were paid for. However, the parent would be reminded by the list to avoid leaving money and credit cards lying around.

A similar list may be useful for keeping track of your teen's constructive, mature actions. It can remind you of the teen's strengths. For example, if your teen practiced his guitar four hours on Saturday and Sunday you would know that the teen has the capacity for 1) concentration, 2) diligence and discipline, and 3) caring. Keeping track of the teen's attributes will make it more difficult to deny the teen's maturity and abilities when a teacher claims the teen has a "short attention span" or the teen seems incapable of cleaning the kitchen.

CONFRONTING DENIAL BY DELAYING THE URGE TO REATTACH

Sometimes a strong urge can be resisted by immediately putting aside the urge and doing something else that brings pleasure. For example, you may feel the need to rescue and comfort your teen who has overslept and is asking for an excuse to miss school for the day. You believe the teen will be more friendly if you cooperate, but sullen for several days if you do not. You can put off the urge to rescue the teen if you decide to gain comfort by calling an old friend that day or seeing a movie. Several hours later, when the teen has gone and you are enjoying yourself, the impulse to take responsibility from the teen for getting to school on time will seem much weaker. Putting off unreasonable requests made by the teen and putting off urges you may feel will give you time to think about the situation: you can gain perspective on the situation when the pressure is off. Delaying urges is called "ratcheting" by Dr. Zev Wanderer (*Letting Go... How to Survive a Lost Romance* and *Make Your New Love Life Better!* by Zev Wanderer and Tracy Cabot). Like a ratchet, it seems difficult to take a stand initially, but then it becomes much easier to hold your position.

Especially, try to delay decisions when you are angry. Do not even enter into a conversation when your temper is out of control. The conversation will turn into an argument or power struggle, and your decisions will be less than optimal. Learn to delay conversations and decisions until you are no longer angry.

CONFRONTING DENIAL BY MAKING CLEAR STATEMENT

Making clear, rational statements of fact can also help prevent denial. "My teen is no longer a child. My teen is a young adult, a capable person. To encourage infantile behavior in my teen is disrespectful of myself and the teen. My teen will not have the opportunity to learn about the real world if I interfere in his affairs by telling his teachers not to discipline him or by paying for the damages he has caused."

Define situations clearly. When the teen says there is no time to do chores, you might say, "You get out of school at 3 p.m. every day and do not have anything to do on Saturday or Sunday. You ARE capable of finding five hours during the week for household chores."

REDEFINE YOUR ROLE TO CONFRONT DENIAL

The effective caretaker, when a child is two years old, is one who is available to satisfy the needs of the child. The effective parent of a teen is one who allows the teen to accept increasing responsibility. The effective parent of a teen will allow the teen to do things without help at appropriate times, and to make some mistakes. The effective parent's role changes over time and with different circumstances. The preschool child needs to be warned of dangers, such as cars and taking candy from strangers. Effective discipline may involve a slap on the bottom or a "time out" in the bedroom. Some teens know more about cars, strangers, and drugs than their parents. After an informative discussion of the dangers and what you will tolerate, consequences that do not involve hitting the teen are needed if there are problems.

CONFRONTING DENIAL BY JOINING A SUPPORT GROUP FOR PARENTS OR TEENS

This will help you fortify yourself. Other parents will confront your denial of the teen's growth and behavior. Since it is usually easier to analyze someone else's problems from a distance, other parents will probably be more objective about your situation than you are. They can offer you support as you go through the stages of mourning.

Be sure to evaluate the advice and help that you get, however. Some parents in groups (and even a few teachers and counselors) push parents to control and protect teens to an unrealistic degree. Some persons, trying to feel superior, attempt to make parents feel guilty about having problems.

Strengthening Your Self

DON'T DENY YOUR NEW IDENTITY

Howard M. Halpern, in the book *How to Break Your Addiction to a Person,* describes how one person's identity is often dependent on a relationship with another person. When relationships end, some people cease to recognize that they can exist as separate persons. Similarly, for years some parents think of themselves as "being a parent." Their daily functions are scheduled around the children's activities (what to buy, where to eat, what TV shows to watch) depend on the children's activities and needs. After many years of basing personal decisions on "the children," some parents find they must make an adjustment in order to make personal decisions based upon their own needs.

Most parents gain satisfaction when their children are friendly and pleasant. The parents know they are functioning well when the children behave and act respectfully. When children become teens, they find other friends, are sometimes moody, and often fail to thank parents for their efforts. A parent who bases personal satisfaction on the teen being friendly, respectful, and appreciative will have periods of personal dissatisfaction.

Many parents judge the success of their day (or of their life in general) on how the kids are getting along. If a mother has three children under five years of age, she may have time for little besides taking care of the kids, and it is only natural to expect the mother to feel better when the children are clean, not crying, and not getting hurt. However, when the children are teens, this same mother may find that some of them will not dress neatly, none will keep their rooms clean, and some of them will not do well in school. If the mother has persisted in judging the success of her functioning in terms of "how well the kids are doing," she may find it impossible to be satisfied with herself. Teens do make independent decisions concerning school, career, and other items. The parents are no longer in control. If the parents base their happiness upon their children's successes, the parents may be frustrated when they cannot control the choices their teens may make that will affect their "success" in life.

Some parents do not feel "whole" by themselves. They have always been a "parent" or "part of a family." Self-respect and satisfaction may be difficult to achieve if a parent denies the possibility that he or she can be a separate, whole person without reference to the existence of ties with others.

Halpern gives sentence completion exercises like the one below. You may think of several ways to complete each statement.

I am...

I was...

I will be...

I like best to...

I deeply believe...

If my teen were to get married and move far away...

Try to see the meaning behind your statements after you have completed the sentences. If your answers suggest that your identity is dependent on your teen's behavior, try to find alternative ways of looking at yourself. For example, you may have said, "I am a parent." Perhaps it would be better to say, "I am a person." Such attempts at self-definition make it more difficult to deny your individuality. Further techniques for strengthening yourself are given in Halpern's book, *How to Break Your Addiction to a Person.* Chapter Seventeen covers in more detail some of the techniques mentioned in this chapter and suggests other exercises for strengthening your sense of identity.

STRENGTHENING YOUR SELF
BY MAKING AN ASSETS INVENTORY

Wanderer (1978) tells how to bolster your self-image in a realistic way by making a list of your personal assets. When you are feeling down or inadequate, make a list of your abilities, personal attributes, and positive features that are not dependent on your children's performances. Keep the list in a private place and update it periodically when you feel the need. The list might include your talents in cooking, dancing, sewing, typing, and business. The list could also include your ability to get along with others, health, and the ability to persevere under pressure. List your material acquisitions, accomplishments, and anything else of which you are proud. The list will be a reminder of your worth and success as a person.

If you find yourself wanting to list negative items about yourself, go ahead. Choose three items that bother you the most and decide what you can *do* about them. Decide not to dwell on guilt or feelings of inadequacy. Just decide if the negative items you listed are worth doing something about or not. If you feel the need to do something about any of these items (e.g., losing weight), make plans to actualize the desired changes. Not only will you feel better about yourself, but you will increase your sense of control at a time when you may feel a loss of control in your family life. You will find that it is possible to make changes in your own life, while forcing changes in your adolescent is often difficult or impossible. This is a reminder that EACH PERSON HAS CONTROL OVER HIS OR HER OWN LIFE, BUT NO ONE ELSE'S.

Techniques for Dealing with Stage Two

Stage Two of mourning involves the intellectual acceptance of separation by teens and parents. Teens may demonstrate attempts at separation by arguing about rules, chores, career choices, politics, and religion. Often these abstract discussions are attempts to show that the teen is a separate, somewhat different person. In reality the teen who is espousing an entirely different value system may still be very emotionally dependent on his or her parents.

Parents who recognize and intellectually accept the maturity of their teens are still faced with a series of decisions concerning how and when to give up control over their teens. Parents at this stage may understand all the changes going on in their family; still, they may find it difficult to actually turn more control over to the teen and to emotionally separate. Turning over control and separating emotionally are best done gradually over the years, as the teen becomes capable of self-control.

IMAGING: AN AID TO ACCEPTANCE OF SEPARATION

Thinking about a situation before it happens can make it easier to understand and accept the situation. Until you have thought through some of the major problems associated with a life change, you will feel uneasy with the change. One way to fortify yourself is to imagine how life could be vibrant, happy, and productive without children. Consider yourself currently in an intermediate situation: the kids are still home, not married, but working at their schoolwork. Even though they are living at home, the teens are thinking, independent individuals.

Visualization of how you can act apart from "being a parent" can be helpful. Such visualizations can provide an intellectual perspective on the changes which are likely to occur in your life as your teens mature. Picture yourself, as if in a vivid dream, in these situations whenever you are upset or need to work out a problem:

a. Alone and making it. Even with the kids not around, you are doing productive work.

b. Alone and in a relaxing area, such as a beach. You can relax and enjoy yourself, even though the kids are not around.

c. Alone and not guilty. Whether doing productive work or simply enjoying yourself, you exist separately from your children without guilt. Perhaps they are doing "well," perhaps not. Responsibility and control go together. As children assume control over their lives, they become responsible for their actions. As your control over the actions of your children decreases, your guilt and worry about their actions becomes ineffective.

PERSPECTIVE BRINGS ACCEPTANCE

A story is told about a note found in the ruins of a building in a Roman city. The note was written by a parent who aggravated herself over her misbehaving teenager. This kid would not keep clean, would not work to earn an apprenticeship, and went with the wrong crowd of people. The parent spent much of her time worrying about the teen, spent much of her money to obtain apprenticeships the teen would not complete, and spent many nights following the teen through the streets in the hope of protecting him from physical danger. Looking back on this note, we can see that two lives were wasted: the teen's and the parent's. The parent gave the teen opportunities for success. But the sacrifice of excessive worry, money, and time doomed the efforts to failure. The parent could have developed her own interests, spent most of her money on what she herself wanted, and avoided ulcers. If left alone, the teen might have gotten tired of running around and settled down. If the mother had refused to provide the nicest clothes and food and unlimited job opportunities, the teen might have started worrying about obtaining these things for himself. Like so many modern parents, some ancient Roman parents devoted much of their allotted time on earth to worrying about and trying to help children who did not appreciate or benefit from their efforts. This story lends perspective to the problems of parent-teen relations. Hopefully it will reinforce an intellectual understanding of the unremitting timelessness of the realities that you and your teen are currently facing.

DISCUSSION FOSTERS ACCEPTANCE OF SEPARATION

Discussions with your spouse or a close friend can help you gain an intellectual acceptance of separation. The discussions can help each of you to understand your marriage, your family, and yourselves. This book, the other books mentioned, and the exercises in these chapters can all be discussed. It is preferable to speak about problems in a planned manner. Discussions about the adolescent can be a mixture of venting your feelings and thought-through observations. There are several concepts, however, that must be kept in mind:

1. Expect Differences of Opinion. You will not see your teen or issues in exactly the same way as your spouse or friend. You each come from different family backgrounds and bring different expectations as to behavior, manners, and accomplishments. Also, teens sometimes act differently around different people. For example, a teen might act appropriately toward one parent but be sullen and moody around the other.

Parents differ in how long it will take them to accept the teen as he or she is. For example, one parent who cares deeply about the teen's future career may push the teen to study, or may accept the teen's story about how the school's inadequacies are responsible for poor grades. The other parent may be more concerned about the teen's lack of motivation to help with housework. Both parents may take a year or two to realize and accept the fact that the teen is not interested in being a college graduate or doing homework.

Acceptance of the teen as he or she is may not come until each parent has tried various solutions, such as explaining to the teen the reason why school is important, examining deficiencies of schools and teachers, and taking care of problems which are apparently bothering the teen. In some cases these efforts are successful: the teen becomes motivated after realizing why school is important, or becomes less distracted after some personal problems are sorted out. In other cases, however, parents eventually realize that their teen is not going to be the star student, athlete, or family member of their dreams.

Learning about, understanding, and coming to accept various aspect's of a teen's personality takes time...often a year or more. To complicate matters, the teen's personality changes with time. No parent will ever be quite up-to-date.

Sometimes one parent has a lack of perspective or misjudges the importance of various factors. For example, a parent may focus attention on grades when the teen's real problem is that he is drunk several days a week. In such as case, seeking treatment for the alcohol problem would be needed before progress with grades could be expected.

2. Stick to Problem Solving. A second consideration to remember when discussing teen problems is to stick to problem solving. Be goal-oriented in your discussions. Blaming each other for mistakes made will not usually help. It is important to avoid attacking your spouse or friend, the school, or the judicial system. There is a lot of room for disagreement, for the reasons discussed above. Even experts differ in their approach to solving any given problem. Perhaps two different strategies would work; there is seldom ONE right answer. Long before the teen years, many children learn how to play one parent against the other. It is easy to have disagreements even without kids' deliberate manipulations. Make a vow not to let kids break you up.

3. Time Limit Discussions. Many discussions are unpleasant. After a full day at work, most of us are not up to a long discussion of the problems the kids have caused during the day. It is easier to handle if an agreement is made to spend five minutes describing the problems, five minutes discussing what might be done about them, and five more minutes deciding what to do. Time limit distasteful and negative discussions.

4. Get Outside Help. Seek counseling if you are not satisfied with the progress you are making or if there is undue friction between you and your spouse. Many counselors are familiar with the types of problems that arise in families with teens. Each situation is different, but there are problems which are common to many families. An experienced counselor can lend perspective on your family's situation. An objective observer can help you gain insight and mobilize constructive change in your family. Remember, seeking professional help is a sign of strength. Seeking counseling demonstrates a desire to grow personally. It is not a sign of failure or weakness. Your old ways of relating may no longer be working. A counselor can help you and your family learn more appropriate ways of parenting.

5. **Save Time for Fun.** Remember to have fun together. It is easy to spend most of the free time you have with your spouse or trusted friend discussing family problems. After an eight-hour work day most people have just a few hours of "alert time" left. If a tense discussion occupies an hour or more of this time, there will be little time for relaxation. Often the tense mood of the discussion lingers on to spoil the time that is left. If such a schedule persists through most of the week, it may seem that you never enjoy seeing your spouse or friend (and vice versa). Especially when a teen is continually acting up, tension can build unless one of the parents remembers to have fun. It is often helpful to say, "Let's go out to dinner and take a walk tonight. We can talk about anything but the kids." Strengthening this relationship can energize you. You will then have the strength and commitment necessary to pursue discussions related to the changes in your child and family.

6. **Take Action.** It is important that your discussions help you devise a strategy for dealing with kid problems. You may need to express feelings, complain, joke, or be sarcastic. These ways of ventilating can relieve some pressure, but they are basically nonproductive. Put a time limit on such conversations. Put the bulk of your time into deciding what to DO. Your teen's behavior will not be changed by talk. It takes action.

You and your spouse or friend can brainstorm. This involves listing as many possible solutions to a problem as possible, without being critical of any solution initially. Later each solution is evaluated.

7. **Agree Upon Bottom Line.** Another process is setting bottom lines, as described in the *Toughlove* books. A bottom line is a limit you set and stick to. Effective bottom lines often involve changing *your* actions, such as giving out privileges, money, favors, and use of the car. For example, you may decide that you will not tolerate being called a "bitch." You decide that you will tell your

teen that you will not cook or do laundry for him for a week each time you are called a bitch. It is fair to inform the teen of your decision and then stick to it. This rule is enforceable: it does not require the cooperation of the teen. Discussion ahead of time helps you to stick to the decision, even if the teen apologizes, promises not to do it again, and so on.

All these tactics will help you get a better intellectual understanding of this stage, bring you closer together, and further strengthen your sense of self. Letting go can then be experienced as an opportunity as well as a crisis.

The Rites of Passage: An Aid to Acceptance of Separation

A book, *The Rites of Passage* by A. Gennep, was first published in 1908 (translated by M.B. Vizedome and G.L. Caffee, University of Chicago Press, 1960). This book discusses culturally defined ceremonies and rituals that existed throughout the world at one time. These events served to mark milestones in the growth and developmental stages of children as they matured. The status of rites was recently reviewed by several counselors (*Rites of Passage in Families with Adolescents* by William H. Quinn, Neal A. Newfield, and Howard O. Protinsky). A summary of their conclusions follows.

In previous generations certain culturally defined and accepted rites of passage were observed by families with adolescents. These rites of passage served to reduce confusion about roles, responsibility, and social position as they changed with the adolescent's age. Many of the rites have been abandoned or modified in character. For example, for thousands of years a Jewish male was considered to have reached a certain level of maturity at age thirteen. When the young man reached this age, he would participate in the reading of the Bible during religious services, a brief reading to be repeated weekly for the rest of the man's life. Taking part in the service was an honor, something which young children did not do. In recent years in many parts of this country the nature of the Bar Mitzvah has changed. Often, a party is put on by the parents. Relatives come from all over the country. Speeches are made, and the teen is expected to perform by reading certain passages. Parents are often put in the position of nagging the child to prepare; thus the emphasis on the child's assumption of responsibility is obscured. Before the Bar Mitzvah many mothers spend months cooking and planning. Seating arrangements at dinner are especially troublesome. Some teens are worried about how they will perform. A very few teens threaten not to go through with the ceremony or get "sick" at the last minute, greatly upsetting their parents. Though the Bar Mitzvah is still a meaningful event for many, it is probably accurate to say that the original meaning of the Bar Mitzvah is obscured a significant percentage of the time.

Teens mature gradually and at different rates. Physical, emotional, social, and intellectual growth do not proceed at the same rate, but they do proceed. Family interactions, responsibilities, and privileges are confused as the teen feels the need for more privileges, but no one is sure if the teen can handle all the accompanying responsibilities. There is no standard protocol or schedule for giving teens gradually increased rights and responsibilities and evaluating their performance. Rites of passage to mark events and accomplishments would be helpful. Sometimes it seems that the only "scheduled" events are achieving the ages at which driving and drinking are permitted. These are given as a reward for living long enough. The concept of being "old enough" to smoke or drink has confused many teens and adults. Graduation from high school and marriage — marks of achievement common to many teens — often come in reverse order. The accomplishment of graduating from high school is noted only as a preliminary step toward college in some families. In other families graduation from college is seen only as a step toward graduate or medical school, and that is only a step toward establishing a thriving business, so that nothing really brings any sense of accomplishment or satisfaction to the child or young adult.

PROVIDING RITES OF PASSAGE

It can be helpful to provide a "rite of passage" for your teen. This rite reinforces both the teen's and the parent's intellectual understanding and acceptance of separation. A practical, dramatic recognition of growth can give the teen confidence, recognition for actual achievements, a sense of acceptance, and a redefinition of responsibility. Old roles are put aside, and new roles are expected. A redistribution of power and responsibility can be accomplished. Old failures can be seen in a positive light. The teen's home environment and attitudes toward the teen can be modified; this will lead to behavioral changes on the part of the teen. For example, the teen who has had a difficult time getting through junior high school can be given a graduation party and shown real respect for the accomplishment. New jobs and household responsibilities with a correspondingly increased allowance can be given. A paying job tutoring younger students could provide confidence and pride as well as a review of previous material. Designing a rite of passage is a difficult task and one that should be personalized to take into account the probable reactions of all family members. Criticism of old rules or an individual's previous performance should be avoided. The entire family's sense of their new reality can be altered in a sincere manner.

The major celebration of a memorable landmark can bring major changes. Similarly, it is possible to show a teen respect and give slight increases in privileges on a weekly or monthly basis. This procedure can gradually improve a family situation.

USING STRESS INOCULATION TO EASE ACCEPTANCE OF SEPARATION

Stress inoculation is a technique described by Dr. Zev Wanderer (1978). Although Dr. Wanderer suggests this exercise for individuals experiencing a relationship breakup, it can also be applied to the parent-teen separation process. The following is a description of how stress inoculation works. Under controlled circumstances people can be given small amounts of a drug to which they are allergic. The body gradually adjusts to it and learns how to take it safely, with no damage. Similarly, you can gradually get used to real and imagined stresses which you fear. It may be that you are upset by things your teen does, or you might be afraid of what he or she will do if you institute changes. For example, you are considering cutting off your sixteen-year-old's allowance because he has not been doing any household chores. In the past when you have tried to institute consequences, he has thrown temper tantrums, sometimes pounding the wall and calling you names. To apply stress inoculation, write down the various things your son might do. Put each one on a separate card. Then, put your cards in order with the least serious action on top. Your cards might read like this:

He will be mad.   He will scream at me.
He will throw a flower pot, break it, and make a mess.
He will tell his grandparents and cause another family feud.
He will be motivated to steal money from my purse.
He will punch the wall and possibly break his hand.
He will punch my jaw and break it.
He will run away from home.   He will kill himself.

Each of these fears are in the back of your mind and might prevent you from carrying out the action you have decided upon, namely taking away your teen's allowance as long as he refuses to do household chores. Thinking rationally about the items on your list, you can see that some of your fears either can be dealt with or are unfounded. You may consider your child too stable to hurt himself. He is too used to the luxuries of home, allowance or not, to run away. You can hide your purse. The grandparents can be told to stay out of the argument. The lesser threats near the top of the list seem more real, though anything is possible. (If some of the fears seem real and insurmountable, get the help of a professional counselor.) In addition to thinking rationally about your fears, practicing stress inoculation can reduce your anxieties and the strain associated with taking a stand.

To practice stress inoculation, lie down and relax. Feel the tension in all parts of your body and release it. Is your forehead wrinkled? Are your arms and legs relaxed? If you have practiced relaxation techniques in the past, you should be able to relax easily. When you feel you are relaxed, read the first card. Think about the event you have written down. Once you have succeeded in staying relaxed with the first card, move on to the second. When you have succeeded in relaxing with this card, move on to the next. By knowing how you will deal with each seemingly possible event and realizing the improbability of the other events, you will be able to relax. It may take some practice, but you will become comfortable with carrying out the decisions you have made.

Techniques for Dealing With Stage Three

Stage Three is the stage of mourning in which the pain of separation is most acutely felt. Grief, depression, and anger are most likely to occur during this stage. The most important thing you can do is to talk about how this new stage in your child's life is making you feel. Parents of even exceptionally well-behaved teens have the fears and feel the losses discussed in the preceding chapters. These parents feel the pain associated with separation also, as their teen matures and moves away.

When a teen acts out, rebels, or has other problems, the separation process is made more difficult and painful. Instead of the separation process taking place smoothly between the teen's ages of thirteen and nineteen (or longer), sudden jolts of realization

strike the parent each time the teen asserts his or her independence. The parent may try to become more controlling, indicating
the difficulty of separation. Working through the mourning process is complicated by fears and guilt. For example, it is more difficult to accept a teen moving out of the home and working at a job
if the parent feels the teen has decided not to go to college because
of mistakes in parenting. A parent in this situation may try to keep
the teen at home or fail to accept the teen who has moved out and is
making it at a decent job. Such a parent may have ambivalent
feelings: love, along with anger at the teen for having made wrong
decisions and hurting the parent.

The grieving process is further complicated when the acting-
out teen and parent are in different stages of separation in regard
to several different issues. For example, a parent would likely have
confused, ambivalent feelings toward a teen who is doing well in a
responsible part-time job but is doing poorly in school. Ambivalent
feelings might be felt for a teen who is developing a pleasing manner and social skills while selling "common" illegal drugs for
extra income.

The parent who experiences ambivalent feelings or guilt
feelings is likely to turn some of his anger inward. Parents may turn
anger toward themselves and feel guilty because of supposedly
inadequate parenting. Anger turned inward leads to depression.

VENTILATION

It is important to find someone you can trust to talk to about your
feelings. This person must keep information confidential. Hurt and
anger need an outlet. Expressing pain and loss can bring relief.
This is different than simply complaining about your teen's latest
antics. Someone is needed to hear your feelings and help you move
past the emotional stage to the stage of acceptance. It is possible to
become addicted to upsetting feelings and to dwell on them too
long.

LIFE REVIEW

It is helpful to review one's past in order to recognize one's
strengths, efforts, and accomplishments. Over time one tends to
forget what really has happened (Robert N. Butler and Myrna I.
Lewis, *Adult Development and Aging*, Little Brown & Company,
1983).

Reconstruct the positive efforts and accomplishments of the

past to gain a clear perspective on the present and future. Part of mourning is reviewing the past and finding its meaning. If you are experiencing problems with your teen, it is natural but self-defeating to look at the teen's problems and say, "It is all my fault. I really was a bad parent." Objectively, look back over the years, review your efforts and activities with the child, and analyze what has happened. You may not be able to pinpoint the sources of the problems, but you will likely see that you did the best you could at the time. Of course, one can always put MORE time into being with the kids, or working to get MORE money for the kids, or reading MORE about how to raise kids, or helping the kids MORE with their homework, or...one can always do more. But, one just does what seems right at the time. A review of your past with this in mind may relieve some unfounded guilt that you are carrying. It may also help you see many of the positive ways that you were there for the child, and how much you really did care for the child.

MANAGING IRRATIONAL GUILT

People with younger children do not always realize it, but once children pass the age of thirteen, they have minds of their own. Question the assumption that you are responsible for the continued misbehavior of your teen.

One way to get rid of the guilt is to try to put into words the reasoning that invokes your guilt. Why DO you feel guilty?

Stop feeling guilty about not having been the perfect parent. You have probably made mistakes in raising your children. Acknowledge these mistakes and make a commitment to change. Accept yourself as a mistake-making human, like everyone else. Realize that people grow by making mistakes. Do not wallow in unproductive guilt. You may say after reading this and other books, "If I had read these books ten years ago, I would not have spoiled my children. I have done irreversible harm to them. I should rot in hell." First, you most likely have done the best you could, given your level of knowledge and models for parenting. Second, you do not have a responsibility to God, your children, or anyone else to be perfect by some book's standards. Third, even if you had read and thought about this and other books, you probably would not have been able to apply the seemingly obvious simple truths they describe. It seems that no matter how much you know and think about a subject, children can go one step beyond your ability to handle it. Take allowances for example. Let's say you decide Jimmy can have an allowance for cleaning up after dinner each night. EXACTLY how much allowance is correct? How imperfectly can the work be done before the allowance should be decreased? How many times should you have to remind him to do it before it is such a hassle that it would have been easier if you had done it yourself? No matter how you answer each of these questions on this "simple" subject, Jimmy may learn of your decision and push you. If you decide a few crumbs on the table and floor are okay, he might leave twice as many and then complain if you don't pay him. Kids are expert at finding out how far you can be pushed before you back down, react, or explode. Even if you know what all the books say about curfew, clothes, money, sex, and every other issue, your kids would find out where you draw the line. And then they might take half a step over the line and try to drag you with them. So...stop your self-criticism due to the fact that you didn't know the "proper" way to raise the kids before. There is no proper way. And if one is found, the kids will find a way around it.

THE ABC's OF GUILT

A theory called Rational Emotive Therapy (*A Guide to Rational Living* by Albert Ellis) says your belief about an action leads to consequences for you. A is an "antecedent behavior" or action. There is a Belief, B, about the Action. The belief determines the Consequences, C. For example:

A. Action: The teen misbehaves.
B. Belief: The parent says, When my teen misbehaves, I have failed.
C. Consequence: The parent becomes depressed and angry.

The goal is to recognize the series of events: A, B, C. It is then possible to change the outcome of the series. In this example, the parent takes control of his or her own thoughts the next time the teen misbehaves, yielding a different outcome:

A. Action: The teen misbehaves.
B. Belief: The parent says, "It is unfortunate he decided to act that way. I did try to teach him differently. I am going to try to teach him differently. I am going to try to help him learn and grow by letting him be responsible for his behavior."
C. Consequence: The parent is not guilty. The teen is not rescued and learns more about the real world.

Another example:

A. Action: Teen calls mother a bitch.
B. Belief: Mother thinks, "Maybe she's right."

C. Consequence: Mother is hesitant to be assertive with the teen and becomes anxious and depressed. Mother taking more care to evaluate the situation:

A. Action: Teen calls mother a bitch.

B. Belief: "My daughter is not showing respect. I will examine my behavior and see if I am acting bitchy, but I will not tolerate such language. I will not take such language personally. If called a foul name, I will not drive, do laundry, or cook for my teen for one week."

C. Consequence: Mother feels better about herself.

THOUGHT STOPPAGE

You will not help your kid by being a martyr. This is destructive behavior. You should socialize and engage in activities you enjoy. When your personal activities are interfered with by thinking or talking about kid problems, set a time limit on how long the thinking or discussion will last, especially when the thoughts are guilty and nonproductive. Say to yourself or your spouse, "We need to talk about this. But, we should be able to decide what we think is right in five minutes. After that I am going to read that mystery book I've been wanting to get to." Time limiting discussions can prevent complex arguments. Time limits tend to give you just long enough to tell how you feel, what you are willing to do, and little else.

Sometimes you will keep thinking about a problem the teen has caused. This constant rumination will interfere with other activities. There is a technique called "thought stoppage": Once you have given the topic all the constructive thought you can, decide you will think about it no longer (or not until the next day, after you have had time to "sleep on it"). Every time you start to think about the problem, forcefully stop the thoughts. Yell, "Stop!" Put it out of your mind immediately. Refuse to think about it. Replace it with pleasant thoughts or plans.

PARADOXICAL INTENT

Paradoxical intent is useful if you are stuck in depression (during Stage Three of mourning) and find it hard to move on to accepting your teen. You may have a hard time trying to ignore your kid's dirty room or the fact you cannot make him come in on time. You may spend much time and energy being angry and worrying about nonproductive issues. One way to realize the worthlessness of worrying about these issues is to assign large doses of nonproductive behavior to yourself. You will quickly tire of the subject, possibly even before you get started.

Consider doing the following:

Sitting home and crying all day about losses.

Breaking up your marriage over the kid.

Being with the kid twenty-four hours a day.

Have a nervous breakdown or develop an ulcer: choose one.

By focusing on the negative results of unproductive thought, you come to realize how bad you can make things for yourself through worry and stress. After deliberately focusing on and practicing upsetting behaviors, you will get tired of it, and you will be more able to proceed positively with your life. Tell yourself that your teen's behavior is obnoxious, and in so many years the teen will be able to leave home. Such thoughts help parents to emotionally detach and focus on developing their own lives. Eventually most teens do become human again.

Summary

Emotionally accepting separation is one of the most difficult tasks you will face as your teen matures. Review what you have done in the past and what you plan to do in the future. Get rid of irrational guilt and stop nonproductive thoughts. These steps will make emotional acceptance of your teen's growth and separation much less upsetting.

Techniques for Dealing With Stage Four

Stage Four of mourning involves detachment and new identification. Letting go is a process of detachment, which leaves you in crisis, even when it occurs gradually over time. In Stage Three you have just mourned for a relationship that is gone forever. You may feel a void. Old meanings are gone, so you must find new meanings. You may go through periods of identity confusion or diffusion. You may feel incompleteness and despair and believe another person is needed to make your life meaningful. Perhaps your spouse, if you have one, has not been able to meet these needs, so you may have tried to derive such meanings from your children. Realize that ultimately only you and the meanings you choose to pursue will give your life value. Develop interests of your own. Get life goals.

The teen changes with maturation. As the adolescent finds a new sense of self and solidifies a new identity, so must the parent. Finding new meaning and purpose in life expands one's personality and growth. Victor Frankl, a psychiatrist who spent many years in a Nazi concentration camp, talks about having a purpose greater than oneself that gives life special meaning. He developed a form of psychotherapy called Logotherapy (therapy concerning meaning). In Logotherapy, people are guided in exploring their values and adding meaning to their lives. Frankl observed that the prisoners who survived the devastating experience of the concentration camps all had some guiding purpose and meaning that got them through the horrible experience. For the camp inmate, this meaning might have been to reunite with a child, spouse, or parent. Having a goal kept the prisoners from depression and even suicide while they were incarcerated. Frankl applied these observations to the general population. He concluded that having a guiding goal or purpose for one's life is a way of combating anxiety and depression.

Depression often occurs when we feel we have no control over what happens. Middle-aged parents often lose control over their own health and figures at the same time that their parents become seriously ill. Parents may also have less control over and success in career goals and be discouraged about life in general. At the same time, teens may also get out of control. Thus, the middle-aged parent may be confronted with loss of control in several areas all at once. Failing to be able to control one's health, career, and parent's health, the urge to control something might lead someone to try to control one's teenage son or daughter. This, however, often turns out to be nonproductive, as we have seen.

Specific goals and activity toward them renews our sense of control over our lives, thereby decreasing the chance of depression. The adolescent transition time is a great opportunity for parents to explore their own values. For the first time in many years they may have time to explore areas that are meaningful to them. As emotional energy is withdrawn from the young child, it can be put into new areas. Howard M. Halpern says that it is important to have multiple attachments in our lives, and suggests ways to find meaning and new connectedness. He speaks of discovering new attachments and meaning in spiritual and social growth, as well as through relating to nature.

The Hindu book *BhagavadGita* presents a similar philosophy.

It says that life has physical, spiritual, and social meaning. Yet, people are led from the true meaning of their lives by day-to-day personal involvements that are not truly important. Only by ignoring daily pressures and mundane activities can one find the true meaning of life. Through meditation or social service, one begins to discover a true purpose in life and the essential unity of all people. Paradoxically, one has to lose oneself in order to find oneself; one needs to ignore personal activities and pressures in order to find the true meaning of one's life and merge with nature. Similarly, the parent of an adolescent has to withdraw from tasks and meanings related to child care that are no longer significant; then the true self of the parent can emerge and be discovered in new meanings and goals. As we make the transition from the task of parenting younger children, however, we may find our lives devoid of a purpose and meaning.

Developing new meaning and transcending the self is especially crucial for single parents who find themselves feeling isolated as their teen matures. A suggestion for parents who are seeking to add connectedness and social concern to their lives would be to start a parent's support group for those who need help coping with their children's adolescence. Parents doing this may gain new friendships, help other people, and grow in their knowledge of teen and community concerns. Much can be done by a group that gets involved in activities such as crisis intervention, community lobbying for counseling services for troubled families, and other significant activities.

A Journey of Aloneness

Some people caught up in day-to-day pressures may find it difficult to rest, think, or find enjoyment. It sometimes helps to get away for a time. This is the purpose of vacations. Unfortunately, vacations for many people have become expensive, stressful, annual excursions, often with the kids along. What some people need is time to rest, be alone, and think about their situation. A day spent at the beach or walking through large city streets can provide you elbow room and enough freedom from immediate pressures to gain perspective on problems and dreams.

Your vacation spot should be a few hours from your home. One day of "vacation" may be all it takes, though you might want to give yourself a weekend or longer. Such trips, if they work for you, will likely be needed every two or three months. These personal journeys will show you that you can get along on your own. They will give you time to reflect upon the spiritual and personal meaning of your life. Often a period of just relaxing is needed before you will be able to constructively think about your "home situation." Observing yourself and others on the beach or in the city is relaxing and can give you food for thought. Perhaps you will be motivated by seeing healthy people on the beach or well-dressed business women in the city. Perhaps the street people in the city will give you perspective on your situation. One mother reported finding inner peace after a stop for coffee and reading before and after work. She took time to relax before work and before returning to the home situation.

Building Self-Esteem

Self-esteem is a sense of your personal worth: the belief that you have value independent of your relationship to others. Before you can build self-esteem, you must ask yourself why your self-esteem needs building and what it would take to build it. Perhaps you do not respect yourself because of poor health, overweight, a low level of educational achievement, or a "nervous condition."

It takes time and effort to change anything of significance in life, and these issues are no exception. You will need time and help in changing any of these important items. Speak to anyone you know who has accomplished what you are seeking. For example, if you know someone who has lost weight or gone back to school in your community, ask them about it. A certain diet, book, school course, or counselor might be needed to start you in the right direction and keep you on track. When trying to change your weight, health, or physical condition, consult your physician about your methods and progress. Improving your physical health can help you move beyond your old self both physically, socially, and spiritually. Feeling better has many positive benefits for you and for your entire family.

Get In Control of Your Life

We often feel out of control when there are too many pressures at once. At certain stages of life we feel a loss of control with our children and family structure. Attempt to gain control in one new area periodically. This will increase your self-esteem. Things will not always go well with changing your habits, your health, or the behavior of your teen. Learn from your mistakes. Try to figure out what went wrong. Then try again, or decide to try something else. Be sure not to develop guilt feelings because you are unsuccessful. See each failure as a positive learning experience. In the following example a parent did succeed in gaining control over certain areas in her OWN life and greatly increased her self-esteem.

Sue had decided to study accounting at night school so that she could get a good job when her children were in school during the day. This meant that for a few years she would have to be at class one night a week and study at other times. After one month of class, she found the house a mess, the bills piling up, and her studies not going well.

Sue felt out of control. She tried to see why things were not working out. Sue had doubts about her ability to do the coursework; she had failed the first examination. Yet, she had done well in high school, and this was a first-year college course. Sue thought about her study time: the kids or the telephone interrupted her at least five times an hour. In college, as Sue's husband had told her, students sit for many uninterrupted hours studying in the library. Maybe interruptions, rather than inability, caused Sue's poor classwork. Sue decided that she would not permit interruptions during her study time. The children would hold their questions and demands until her study hour was finished each night, unless there was a real emergency (like a broken arm). The children would take telephone messages for mom, rather than mom answering the phone...most of the calls were for the kids anyway.

The problem with bills piling up had two causes: Sue's husband was out of town a lot or was too busy to process the paperwork. And, there was not enough money for some of the bills to be paid. Sue hated to have to face the bills. She felt she could not tolerate working on them for more than one hour a week. So, Sue put aside one hour a week to work on bills, again insisting that she not be interrupted during this time. Sue found that if she really applied herself, she could make progress. She made arrangements to make small payments on some of the bills that had been overdue. She found ways to reduce some bills: the air conditioner and lights were to be used less and there would be more chicken than steak.

Do Things for Others

Many people find satisfaction in helping others. Your self-worth may be increased if you lend a hand to people in need. We are not talking about doing more for people who do not appreciate your efforts. We are talking about helping people who need and want help. There are many volunteer positions involving reading for the blind, church work, helping in hospitals, tutoring students who want help, working in the school or city library, and helping in nursing homes. You may not find the human contact you need in positions in which you simply collect money. Look for a position that enables you to help someone directly. The rewards will be more than you expected. In addition, you will get out, meet people, and learn about organizations and your community. This is an example of how you can become socially active and effective.

Enjoy yourself

Engage in nondepressing behavior. You will not help your teen by being a martyr. This is destructive. It is normal to want to socialize and engage in fun activities. Sometimes you will be prevented from enjoying yourself because you are worried about what others may think. Perhaps your parents or the neighbors are giving you a guilt trip about your kid's behavior. Perhaps you experience daily upsets at seeing the house littered by the kids. Determine what it is that is upsetting you. Search out your vulnerabilities and decide what to do about them. This search may require that you ask a friend or a counselor for help in analyzing your situation. It may require that you take a vacation. Whatever it takes, do it. You may be afraid of other's opinions, or of losing your kid's love when you take a firm stand. If so, you need to work on your vulnerabilities.

Decide What It Is You Want Out of Life

If you have never considered it before, it might sound strange, but many people never stop to think about their life goals. The goal-setting process of many people is more like stumbling through life: get through school, get married, get a house or apartment, get a car, have kids, do what you have to do.

Dreams and goals seem to be reserved for kids: being an

astronaut or movie star are unrealistic dreams for most people, but these are the last dreams many parents have had...except for the dreams and hopes they have for their kids.

It helps to get your life in order if you think about what you really want to do with your life. One way to do this is to think about what you would do if you knew you had only one month to live. Some top priorities would show themselves, though they are things you have probably been putting off entirely. Think about what you WOULD do if you had only one or six months to live. Make concrete plans to fulfill what you want out of life and go for it. Get the support of your spouse if you are married.

YOUR LIFE

Your life is important. Do something with it. Check your progress daily using the checklist below.

Daily Checklist

1. Do I know (or am I working on finding) my health and career goals for the next five years?
2. What did I do yesterday, and what will I do today to come one step closer to my goals?
3. Is anything interfering with my goals? What can be done about this?

Summary

Stage Four of mourning involves detachment and new identification. Techniques helpful in Stage Four include finding new meaning in life, building self-esteem, getting in control of your life, learning from your mistakes, engaging in nondepressing behaviors, deciding what you want out of life, and making a daily checklist.

Techniques for Dealing with Stage Five

Stage Five of mourning involves the teen and parent developing mature ways of relating to each other. This permits them to grow, develop personal strengths, and choose interests to pursue in life. Techniques which are helpful in developing mature relationships include coming to terms with your own imperfections, practicing assertiveness, demanding respect from others, and considering yourself and your teen to be equal in worth.

COMING TO TERMS WITH YOUR IMPERFECTIONS

Many people find it difficult to respect themselves or bolster their egos when they know they have obvious defects. Some parents have their imperfections pointed out to them by their teens. For example, on various occasions one mother tried to tell her daughter not to smoke, drink, or have sexual relations until she was married. Whenever such subjects were brought up, daughter reminded mother that she smoked, had at least one beer a day, and stayed out "awfully late" on many of her own dates (the mother was divorced). When confronted by her own imperfections, the mother always backed down and became confused and depressed.

There are a number of things you can do when confronted with your imperfections. First, tell your teen that you are not perfect, but you did want the teen to know you consider it harmful to do the behavior in question. Second, try to modify your behavior. Perhaps you need to see a physician about nicotine gum, which makes it easier to stop smoking. Consider joining a weight loss program. Go to Alcoholics Anonymous if you really cannot stop drinking. No one is perfect. However, you must also consider that it is now time to stop lecturing your teen. In this stage you are relating in an adult-to-adult manner. You might express concern and caring if you are worried about your teen, but this is definitely a time to treat the teen as you would an adult friend. Remember: you deserve to be treated with the same respect.

Also, remember that the rules for teens and adults are not always the same: the law simply may not allow teens to drink or stay out late. For example, one parent told his sixteen-year-old to obey the curfew law. The teen replied that the law was stupid, and she probably would not be arrested anyway. The parent gave the teen responsibility by saying, "I would like you to follow the law. If you do get picked up for violating curfew, I will not come in the middle of the night to take you out of the detention center. I will not tell the police that you forgot just this once and I expect you will follow the curfew in the future. You are on your own regarding this issue."

BE ASSERTIVE

Practice assertiveness. This means being in charge of your own life, having confidence in your own judgment, being firm while keeping your temper, and insisting on your rights as well as the rights of others. It is desirable to avoid aggression and passivity. Books on the subject of assertiveness include *Stand Up, Speak Out, Talk Back* by Robert E. Alberti and Michael L. Emmons (Pocket Books, New York, 1975) and *Don't Say Yes When You Want To Say No* by Herbert Fensterheim and Jean Baer (Dell Books, New York, 1975).

DEMAND RESPECT FROM OTHERS

An important part of being assertive is demanding respect from others. Do not listen to nagging, complaints, or screaming. Just stick to your reasonable demands. Exactly how to do this is described in the books by Kiley, the *Step-Teen* and *Toughlove* books, and the books on assertiveness. What lines to draw, demands to refuse, and limits to put on discussions depends on how you feel and on how your teen is acting.

Some parents find arguments and a show of disrespect to be quite upsetting. Actually, we all have our limits. After living over a decade with you, your teen knows how to find and lean on your limits. For example, when there is a disagreement, some discussion is always reasonable. But how much explanation, compromise, and discussion is tolerable?

We all have very different frustration limits, and you must recognize your own. Some of these differences came about because of the way you were introduced to stress, arguments, and conflict as a child. While writing this book, we were driven through downtown Boston during rush hour on a Friday afternoon by a young lady who worked in a car rental agency. She noticed people edging into her lane and trying to cut her off, but she held her ground and did not get upset. She was unaffected by a number of close calls which would have upset either of us, had we been driving. We asked her how long she had been driving in Boston. She replied that she had LEARNED TO DRIVE only a few months before. She had never seen the courteous drivers of the midwest or the cursing, honking drivers in New York City. She was just used to, and accepting of, the many tight merges necessary in Boston.

You may not be able to change your tolerance for discourteous treatment, arguing, invasion of your privacy, or stretching of rules.

But take action instead of becoming emotionally upset when you are treated poorly. Rather than getting hooked into endless arguments, simply hold your ground and state your position. Stick up for your rights, but do not lash out. In technical terms, be assertive, but not aggressive. Stay in your lane and smoothly allow your teen to merge with your needs and abilities. Do not get sucked into fights or arguments. Just state your limits and the consequences that will result if they are not respected. After you have explained your limits and listened to your teen's response, you may need to remove yourself from the scene in order to avoid further argument, disrespect, or mistreatment.

CONSIDER YOURSELF EQUAL TO YOUR TEEN IN WORTH

Using assertiveness to maintain a sense of equality is important in parentteen relationships. You may think you consider yourself equal in importance to your children, but chances are you do not act that way. Are you really treating yourself as an equal? Consider the following questions as being relevant to this point:

Do the teens do as much cooking, laundry, and housework as you?

Do the teens have more free time than you do, and how do they use it?

Do you drive teens in carpools and then not have time for your own recreation?

Do you hesitate to take a course in school because you will not have time to help the teens with their homework?

Do you spend time driving your children to (or watching them play) sports, while you are out of shape?

Do you spend as much time developing your own career and education as you do helping your teen with his or hers? Remember that time spent on another's career is sometimes wasted.

ACT AS IF

It is not too difficult to read through this chapter. However, most people take several years to *Apply* the principles and techniques described here, even if they know and understand the material. There are several reasons for this. First, it is difficult to recognize areas in one's own life that need changing. This is why discussions with one's spouse, a friend, or a counselor can help. Second, it is difficult to change one's own feelings, habits, beliefs, dreams, and behaviors.

There are several techniques which will help you change your feelings and behaviors. Imaging has already been mentioned: take time to imagine yourself looking and acting differently. Think of how things could be. An extension of this technique is to ACT AS IF you have already succeeded in your goals. Add one goal at a time. For example, you might start acting as if you were not used to profane language or littering in your home. You would then find it easier to enforce consequences when such problems were encountered. You might ACT AS IF you did have a half an hour every morning to exercise and another half hour in the afternoon to read poetry. You would act this way even if the laundry were not done, the house cleaning were not finished, and the "best" meal were not prepared for dinner.

ACT AS IF you are an important, worthwhile person who is worthy of respect. Acting "as if something is true" helps you to really believe it. Strongly felt beliefs tend to spread to other people.

6 Assessing Your Teen's Behavior

Courage is not the absence of despair;
it is, rather, the capacity to
move ahead in spite of despair.
— *Rollo May, Psychoanalyst*

There are hundreds of books on how to teach, raise, and discipline children. Proposals in these books vary from holding children accountable for their behavior to buying them computers. The suggestions may be appropriate for certain teens in certain situations, but how does a parent know what to do at any specific time? The answer is that to be effective a parent's behavior must take into account the teen's behavior and the parent's own needs and feelings. For example a rational discussion of a problem is supposed to be an effective way to resolve it, but a rational discussion of a problem can be expected to be ineffective if the teen is too angry or intoxicated to discuss the problem. Similarly, a parent who tries to fake a rational discussion while actually seething with anger over the teen's behavior is also going to be ineffective. At times a parent will not realize that he or she is angry. For instance, Tom had not been doing his chores around the house, though he kept promising he would. Tom wanted his mother to pick him up from a dance at midnight. Tom's mother said she did not want to stay up that late. They could not come to an agreement on a time suitable to both of them. The real reason an agreement could not be reached was that, although she did not realize it, Tom's mother did not want to give Tom a ride at ANY time because she was angry that he was not doing his chores. Tom's mother was not in touch with her feelings. She just had a vague sense that she did not want to stay up late in order to do Tom favors.

New Ways of Interacting Are Often Needed

The interaction you have with your teen naturally changes over the years. At first your child is completely dependent upon you for feeding, burping, and diaper changing. Eventually, your child will be living away from you and making family and career decisions without asking your opinion. Somewhere between these two extremes are the "teen years." Most parents have preconceived ideas and dreams for their children's school, athletic achievements, careers, and marriages. And, many parents hope eventually for grandchildren. Most parents dictate or strongly influence their preteen's decisions concerning dress, eating, church attendance, study habits, curfew, and friends. Telling a teen what "should" be done often becomes ineffective when the teen wears sloppy clothes, eats mostly potato chips, decides the church is a waste of time, does not feel a need to study, wants to stay out late, and has friends who are getting in trouble. New ways of interacting with the teen are needed.

Factors Which Influence Methods of Interaction

Many books explain how to discipline, control, and otherwise interact with teens. This book offers advice on how to choose methods of interaction in various situations from existing books and provide some additional interactional techniques. Many behavioral methods are appropriate...there is no one correct way.

How you can effectively interact with your teen (or anyone else) depends on many factors. These factors include the feelings, beliefs, trust, and desires of you and your teen. Many books suggest family negotiations during the teen years, but if either person in a discussion is angry, little in the way of complex negotiations will be accomplished. This may be an ideal time to express feelings of hurt and anger, however; negotiations can be started later. If the parent believes it is possible to retain control over a teen's career values, friction will come if the teen makes choices that do not agree with the parent's. If a parent does not trust a teen to follow through with an agreement, a deadline for its accomplishment should be indicated, and consequences for failure to keep the agreement are needed. Most books have suggestions for building trust, and this is quite important. At times parents will be too hurt to feel trust for the teen and will concentrate on gaining compliance instead.

At times you may be able only to enforce consequences but not feel love or trust for your teen. Do not feel guilty about your feelings. Trust comes with time and must be earned. Feelings of hurt and anger are normal after trust has been betrayed. If there are long-standing problems, it will take time for you and your teen to rebuild trust and your relationship. Trust can be "given" only so many times; then it must be earned. For example, Fred had several minor accidents wile driving. His father wanted to restrict Fred's driving to the daytime because the accidents occurred at night. Fred said he was angry because his parents did not "trust" him. Fred's mother convinced her husband to allow Fred to drive at night. Fred had more accidents, and eventually the court took his license away. Misplaced trust can be harmful.

Sometimes compliance will come from the parents being more flexible: if a teen is feeling a need to obtain self-control, suggestions made by parents may be rejected simply because they were made by the parents. Giving some choice and flexibility may help a teen take responsibility and enjoy it. For example, a teen may feel respected and powerful if allowed to choose exactly when and how a chore will be done rather than having all the details dictated. Flexibility is desirable in most relationships, but there are practical limits, especially when the teen is insincere. John, for instance, said he would pay for the tools he lost within a month. Although he continued to spend money on dates and records, the money was not paid back. When he asked for an extension of the time for paying his debt, his parents were appropriately inflexible.

At times, parents will do better by letting the teen be solely responsible for his or her actions. This often occurs when the school imposes consequences on the teen and the teen asks the parents to intervene.

A teen will change behavior with time, having what has been called "ups and downs" or "going through stages." Problems may seem to disappear, only to recur over time. Sometimes parents can understand why the teen is changing: peer influence or pressures, too much free time, or a natural desire to be independent and in control. At other times parents do not know what "has gotten into" their teen; they just know they are having difficulty dealing with the situation. Sometimes a teen will have problems in one area, yet be doing well in others. For example, Bob fought with his parents constantly while getting along with his teachers at school. Alice got along well with her mother but was suspended repeatedly from school. At any given time a teen can be in different stages of development or difficulty in various life areas.

The chart below describes general degrees of difficulty which can be experienced. The number of levels or stages is arbitrary...there can be three or five stages of difficulty. The important thing is that you realize there are different stages. In each stage different ways of interacting with the teen are needed. The martial (fighting) arts recognize the need to take into account the actions of others. In Aikido, especially, one's actions are dictated by the actions of the opponent. In business, sports, and human interactions of all kinds it is desirable to modify one's actions and strategies to take into account the behavior of others. Teen's exhibiting different behavioral patterns must be dealt with in different ways.

Stage	Degree of Difficulty	Description
1	None	Well adjusted. Cooperates and enjoys it. Few long-lasting disagreements.
2	Mild	Mild adjustment problems. Breaks some rules, but readily cooperates with reasonable discipline.
3	Moderate	Repeatedly breaks rules or laws involving drugs, alcohol, sex, or curfew.
4	Severe	Habitually violent, drunk, on drugs, or not in control.

Table 6-A. Teen Behavioral Patterns

A teen in Stage 1 usually has goals which coincide with those of the parents, or just has not thought about doing anything differently than has always been expected. Many teens do fit into this category, but if your child did you probably would not be reading this book.

There seems to be a large gap between Stages 2 and 3 as they are described in the table. However, many parents who have thought their teen was in Stage 2 suddenly find the teen has been in Stage 3 for many months. Some parents with teens clearly in Stage 4 do not recognize (or deny to themselves as well as others) that their teen is in serious trouble.

Make Interactions Match Your Teen's Stage

If your teen is truly in Stage 1 (no difficulty), you need to continue to teach responsibility and encourage character growth. You probably won't have any trouble if you are sincere and treat the teen with respect. In Stage 2 the important word is "reasonable" discipline. This is a complex subject about which many books have been written. One of the best books is *Step-Teen*, which describes interactions, agreements and negotiations in great detail.

As teens move from Stage 2 to Stage 3 they sometimes lose the ability or desire to negotiate, discuss or be truthful. Additional parental skills, such as those described in the *Toughlove* series of books, are needed in Stage 3. The problems described in the next chapter are encountered in Stages 3 and 4. In Stage 4 it is physically dangerous to allow the teen to stay at home. Drug and alcohol rehabilitation programs and the issues discussed in the chapter on legal matters become relevant.

KNOW YOUR TEEN'S STAGE

It is difficult to be objective when evaluating your self, and sometimes more difficult to be objective when evaluating your own child. However, it is useful to categorize your teen's behavior into the Stages listed above. Your teen's behavior and Stages will change with time. Your teen may seem to exhibit characteristics of several Stages at once. Nevertheless, it is worthwhile to evaluate your teen's Stage because this will influence your discipline methods and let you know when outside help is needed. Outside assistance is definitely needed in Stages 3 and 4, and rarely needed in Stages 1 or 2.

STAGE 4: SEVERE PROBLEMS

Parents sometimes fail to recognize when their teens are in Stage 4. Often, there is denial, an unconscious failure to recognize signs of trouble or to realize what they mean. Ask yourself the following questions. Any "yes" answers mean you are in Stage 4 and in need of a professional counselor.

Questions Which Indicate Stage 4

1. Has your teen intentionally struck you because he or she was angry with you?
2. Is your teen drinking alcohol or taking recreational drugs daily?
3. Has your teen missed several days of school this year because of drinking or taking drugs?
4. Are you afraid of your teen?

STAGE 3: MODERATE PROBLEMS

In Stage 3 your teen repeatedly engages in illegal behavior. It is difficult to recognize and label a teen as being in Stage 3 because society may sanction such behavior. You, as a parent and an individual, must decide what is right and wrong. Some parents see nothing wrong with a teen drinking alcohol every weekend as long as it does not interfere with school or driving. Other parents would see such drinking patterns as early signs of alcoholism. While some issues are debatable, others are not. We believe that a "yes" answer to any of the questions below means that your teen is in Stage 3. This means that you need professional counseling. Also, you need to employ the disciplinary methods described in the *Toughlove* books and the next chapter of this book.

Questions Which Indicate Stage 3

1. Has your teen been selling illegal drugs?
2. Does your teen repeatedly sneak out after curfew (despite your willingness to let him or her stay out until the legal curfew and sleep at friends' houses where parents are present)?
3. Have there been two occurrences in the last six months in which your teen was found to be:
    A. using alcohol or other drugs
    B. missing school
    C. staying out beyond curfew without a good excuse
    D. engaging in promiscuous sexual intercourse OR
    E. being in fights in which medical treatment was needed

STAGES 1 AND 2

Even if your teen is not in Stages 3 or 4, the information about Stages 1 to 4 in the table will help you recognize trouble signs in your teen and other teens. Recognizing trouble in a friend of your teen is not necessarily grounds for forbidding your teen to associate with that person. First, your teen may learn from seeing the mistakes of others and the effects of those mistakes. Second, your teen may help the troubled teen. Third, it is usually impossible to totally control a teen's choice of associates.

Summary

Learn to evaluate your teen's degree of behavioral difficulty. The teen's stage of difficulty will change over time. It is important to know where your teen stands so that you can get outside help when it is needed, employ proper disciplinary methods, and evaluate your progress. The next chapter discusses general effective interaction and disciplinary techniques as well as specific teen problems and how to deal with them. You cannot directly change your teen's behavior. You can only change YOUR behavior. As discussed in the next chapter, changes in your behavior make the teen's behavior easier to tolerate and can sometimes cause the teen to act differently.

How Your Feelings Can Help You Deal with Your Teen's Behavior

7

This chapter shows how ignoring your feelings can interfere with effective child raising and lead to further unhappiness for you. Self-defeating parental feelings include bitter disappointment, guilt, hopelessness, and denial. This chapter focuses on parental feelings in terms of discipline. Choosing (and periodically modifying) a general strategy of discipline, rather than unique disciplinary methods, is stressed. Entire books have been devoted to the subject of how to discipline and raise teens. Rather than duplicate the information found in these books, we will refer you to the appropriate references. Your use of these references will vary with the time, the particular situation, and the stage (degree of teen difficulty. Among the best of the books on child and teen discipline are:

Keeping Kids Out of Trouble by Dan Kiley. This book most clearly explains how to teach young children discipline and respect for others. Kiley tells how to deal with infants, toddlers, and children of all ages up through the teens. How children learn disrespect and how to manipulate parents is illustrated with all-too-common examples.

Step-Teen (Systematic Training for Effective Parenting of Teens) by Don Dinkmeyer and Gary D. McKay. This is a detailed, clearly written manual which explains how to: establish meaningful relationships with teens, understand a teen's motives and feelings, decide which problems should be left for the teen to solve and take responsibility for alone, and how to discipline teens in general.

Toughlove by Phyllis and David York and Ted Wachtel. This book tells how to deal with a severely acting-out teen who does not respond to the methods in *Step-Teen*. The teen described here does not respond to explanations, fairness, understanding, and shows of unqualified love. This may occur because the teen had the methods of *Step-Teen* applied too late or because of outside influences such as peers or relatives. Many parents find it best to mix or combine the methods of *Step-Teen* and *Toughlove*, depending on the situation.

The Peter Pan Syndrome by Dan Kiley. While this is not a book on child raising, it does describe teens and adults who have never learned responsibility or grown up. Teens who are not given responsibility gradually can become Peter Pans.

Toughlove Cocaine by Phyllis and David York. This is a manual which helps parents and others living with an addict to break through the denial concerning the person's drug habit. Addicts, including people who drink alcohol daily, need professional help. People who live with addicts may put up with a lot rather than force the addict to get help. *Toughlove Cocaine* focuses on the decision to get professional help.

How to Choose Child Rearing and Discipline Methods

Hundreds of books, including those listed above are available that tell how to raise children. Each book can be evaluated according to the degree of teen difficulty that is being addressed. For example, the *Step-Teen* book is most useful in dealing with teens who can be reasoned with. These teens fall into the Teen Behavioral patterns listed in Chapter Six as Stages 1 and 2 (none or mild degrees of acting out). The *Toughlove* book can be thought of as being of more use for the teen with moderate behavioral difficulty (Stage 3 — repeatedly breaks rules or laws involving drugs, alcohol, sex, or curfew). If one's teen is a drug addict (Stage 4 — severe difficulty), the *Toughlove* and *Toughlove Cocaine* books are needed, along with professional help.

Of course, there is overlap. For example, many of the *Step-Teen* principles apply to the *Toughlove* or Stage 3 teen. And, teens change their apparent degree of behavioral difficulty from day to day or when different topics arise.

In general, parents feel and try to show concern and love for their teens. Parents try to give teens as much freedom and choice as possible. When the teen does not cooperate or does things which are potentially harmful or improper for some reason, parents may give up their ideals of freedom and choice for the teen and may feel betrayal, lack of trust, disappointment, and frustration. Therefore, a parent's feelings are one guide to the effectiveness of a child rearing or discipline method. When one method of interaction does not work, another must be tried if there is to be change. The story of Pete given below provides many examples of unsuccessful methods of dealing with problems. Alternative solutions that might be tried for various problems are described. The fact that there is no one proper way to handle any given problem makes it difficult to say what the proper parental response to any problem "should" be. Too many couples are torn apart by arguments over how a teen problem should have been handled. Parents spend much time arguing over teen issues instead of loving each other, enjoying life, and following career or personal goals. Note how Pete's parents are driven from each other from time to time in the story below.

The most important point to remember when handling teen problems is that *you must know and understand your own feeling.* If you find yourself arguing with your spouse after wanting to see him or her all day, stop to consider what is happening. If you feel angry, cheated, or betrayed by the actions of your teen, take time to analyze the situation.

Teens have their ups and downs. They will be cooperative one day and moody the next. Peer pressures and suggestions made by well-meaning but meddling adults may make the once-satisfied teen become unhappy with privileges, curfew, or allowance. Parents often do not have the energy to investigate or adapt to these changes. Often a change comes after someone has tried to "rescue" the teen from a difficult situation. For example, Sue accidentally ripped two of her fairly new sweaters and burnt holes in two more with cigarettes. Sue's parents told her that she would have to earn money for new sweaters by doing extra work around the house or by getting a part-time job at a place of her choice. Sue found several friends and relatives who were willing to give her sweaters. Sue told friends that her parents were refusing to buy her clothes. She told one of her aunts that she saw some clothes that would make a nice present for her next birthday. No one but Sue realized what was occurring. Sue was learning how to circumvent her parents' wishes and the natural consequences of her own carelessness with clothes. Teens can often find people to rescue them from consequences imposed by nature or their parents. While most people who help teens out of a tough situation may be unaware of the cause for the teen's distress, others do know they are rescuing the teen.

Teens often *vary* in their degree of cooperation, referred to in the last chapter as degree of behavioral difficulty. For example, a teen may follow curfew rules and do well in school, yet refuse to do chores around the house.

Most parents have strong feelings, hopes, expectations, and dreams for their children. Many parents judge the success of their lives on how well their children do. Our culture, legal system, and major religions support and encourage this attitude. Books and computer programs for teaching children are much more prominent in bookstores and magazines than are educational or vocational materials for adults. Legal information about parent-child relationships says little about the rights of parents. Instead, the legal literature is mostly concerned with the rights of children, protecting children from various abuses or legal consequences, and offering ways to obtain legal custody and child support payments. The same can be said of the psychological and developmental literature. This is good, necessary material, but there is a need for balance! The Bible speaks repeatedly of rewarding the children and descendants of an individual, rather than rewarding the individual himself ("Your seed will multiply and occupy this land...").

Parents often start making plans for their children before they are conceived. During pregnancy, books and educational toys are bought. Plans are made which will lead to the Nobel Prize or a position in a big league baseball team. A great deal of time, money, and emotional energy is invested over the years in the child's "life" or "future." During childhood, parents are concerned about their child's learning, exercise, weight control, and talents. Yet parents often, at the same time, ignore their own accomplishments in these areas. Parents may sit many hours a week watching their children play baseball in expensive uniforms. Yet these same parents may be overweight and in poor health. Time may be spent driving children to expensive music, dancing, and computer lessons while the parents "don't have the time or money" to invest in their own career development and health.

Many children stay in Stage 1 of behavioral difficulty (few problems) until age eight or ten. Then the child gains the ability to make choices and develop interests of his or her own choosing. By this time the parents have spend a decade dreaming about and working toward developing the child's education, sports ability, health, career, and "future." This has often been at the expense of the parent's personal development. When the teen or pre-teen loses interest in sports or schoolwork, parents are often disappointed. In time the disappointment can develop into hurt and even anger.

Be in touch with your feelings! If you feel disappointment in your teen, analyze why. Are you holding your teen to the standard of your dreams? Are you hurt because you spent so much time driving to little league practices? Are you upset because your teen is making life choices which may not lead to the "best" career? Parents often try to "help" their teen follow the right path, giving unwanted help with homework, paying for grades earned, and generally trying to keep the teen out of trouble. Parents often feel betrayed when their offspring seem to rebel against family, religious, and social values. The following story describes one such family.

The Story of Pete

Mary and George met in college. After graduation, they married, and George became a department store manager. Mary had never wanted a career. She wanted to have a family and be a mother. Within a year after George and Mary married, they had Peter. They read to him, talked to him, watched Sesame Street with him, and took him to museums...long before he could talk. In grade school Pete took music lessons and played in the little league. Pete's grandparents lived a few miles away and visited him nearly every week. In general, they praised him and gave him presents. At first Pete's parents were pleased with the extra babysitting help, but after Pete was about six years old they felt they were competing with both sets of grandparents. If Pete was told he could not stay up late or go to a movie, he would say that his grandparents would let him do it. If his parents said they did not want to buy him a new toy or sweater, Pete would get the grandparents to buy it. Pete's parents wanted Pete to learn how to take care of and appreciate the value of what he had. They wanted him to earn money and save it before obtaining large items such as color televisions and computers. Even though Pete's parents explained these wishes to the grandparents, Pete was able to convince the grandparents to buy him what he wanted. For his birthday one year, Pete received a color TV *and* a computer. Pete's parents felt handicapped in teaching Pete to care for his belongings and in teaching him the value of money because of the grandparents' gifts. Pete knew this and would make use of the situation in later years. George and Mary could have confronted both sets of grandparents but did not want to "cause trouble." George and Mary felt uncomfortable with the situation but did nothing about it. George and Mary were not assertive with either generation. This was destructive to Pete. He learned that he could manipulate his parents and use his grandmother to bail him out of difficult situations.

When he entered junior high, Pete started to spend much of his free time with a group of boys who enjoyed video games and movies. Pete's parents were disappointed when Pete's music teacher said that Pete was not longer making progress. Pete no longer practiced, and even missed some lessons. His parents made a chart for Pete to fill in, showing how much time he practiced. Pete wrote in an hour each day, but his parents never heard him practice. Pete's mother wanted to offer to pay Pete to continue practicing and going to lessons, saying it was work for which Pete was receiving no pay. Pete's father wanted to charge Pete for the lessons he had missed which still had to be paid. Pete's parents discussed this for several weeks. The discussions turned into arguments. Both parents felt out of control of the situation, and neither felt emotionally close to the other after the arguments, which occurred almost daily.

Mary and George did not realize that Pete's music was his concern — a "his life item" as described in *Step-Teen*. Although his parents had invested dreams and money in music lessons, Pete's dropping music would not really affect his parents. Eventually Pete's parents did increase his allowance on the condition that he continue the lessons. Pete continued the lessons for about three months, and then got into arguments with the instructor and refused to take any more lessons. When his parents said they would reduce his allowance, Pete threatened to do poorly in school.

Pete claimed that his "work" and contribution to the family was his schoolwork. Pete felt he deserved an allowance, clothes, rides, and everything else "good parents gave all the other kids." His only responsibility was to do well in school. Pete claimed he "needed" money for dates, records, tapes, and concerts. When he did not have enough, he would take small amounts of money from his parents' bedroom. Though he did not admit to taking any money when his parents asked specifically about missing cash, they suspected Pete was stealing. He became quite angry when asked about stealing and retaliated by telling his grandparents about how deprived he was. Sympathy, gifts (including money), and a plea to Pete's parents to "stop making him neurotic" resulted. Endless discussion followed because George thought Pete should get a part-time job to earn his spending money, while Mary thought he should have a larger allowance. George and Mary felt they were drifting apart, unfairly judged by their own parents, and not in control of their home situation. But they did nothing about their feelings.

Pete felt he was misunderstood, unloved, and not wanted by his parents. Despite his role in this struggle, Pete was unhappy. Pete was discouraged by his parents' mounting resentment and emotional distancing. Pete's parents were concerned, but expressed this concern by telling Pete what they thought he should do. Pete did not want to hear this. He could have been given respect for taking responsibility and doing jobs around the house. *Step-Teen* tells how to initiate such actions, and they would have helped at this point. *Step-Teen* also tells how to be sensitive to teen's motivations, such as revenge, feelings of inadequacy, or needs for power. Specific exercises are given for dealing with revengeful behavior and lack of cooperation. Pete's parents needed to negotiate for privileges: they were giving him an allowance, driving him around town, doing his laundry, and getting little in return. *Step-Teen* tells how to initiate and carry through negotiations that put living arrangements on a more even footing. *Toughlove* tells how to accomplish such negotiations with the older or more independent teen or young adult who is not so dependent on daily favors, that can be used in bargaining. The teen who is willing to discuss a situation and come to an agreement can usually be dealt with using *Step-Teen* techniques. When rational discussions and agreements cannot be made or adhered to, *Toughlove* methods become more useful.

NOT SEEING THE OBVIOUS: DENIAL

Pete did feel close to friends his own age. Like many teens these days he experimented with drugs, especially alcohol and marijuana. Pete was able to hide this from his parents because he would only get drunk or stoned when "sleeping over" at a friend's house. When Pete came home tired and irritable from sleepovers, his parents assumed it was because the boys had stayed up too late.

Mary and George heard stories from several friends about

drinking parties and drug use. When they asked Pete about these, Pete became quite angry. He said that his parents had made his life at home miserable, and that they wanted to ruin his social life as well. Pete denied using any drugs or alcohol, though he admitted that several of his friends knew people who used drugs on occasion. Pete's parents were satisfied with this explanation until they found pipes for smoking marijuana in Pete's room. Again they confronted him. Pete said that the pipes were for experimenting with tobacco and other "natural herbs."

Pete's father was sure he was using drugs because of the stories they had heard, Pete's falling grades, his moods, and his inability to save money despite a large allowance. Also, jewelry, alcohol, money, and other valuables were disappearing from the house. Pete was taken to the family's physician. He examined Pete and spoke to him. The doctor found nothing wrong, but recommended seeing a counselor. Pete did not want to see a counselor. His father did not want to pay for a counselor. Pete's mother did not believe Pete was using drugs; she strongly believed that Pete would never do anything seriously wrong.

Some common reasons for avoiding counseling are illustrated here. The person who needs it the most is usually fearful of change. The person who is responsible for payment does not want to pay. There is often denial on the part of each family member concerning the need for counseling.

RESCUE FROM A CRISIS

Pete's one interest which his parents hoped might lead to a career was auto mechanics. Pete spent much of his time helping his friends fix their cars. Though his parents did not approve, his grandparents gave Pete a car when he was sixteen. His grandparents felt they were contributing to his future...Pete had convinced them he intended to attend auto mechanics' school after graduating from high school.

Pete refused to buy insurance for the car, so his father felt he had to. Pete had several small accidents which always seemed to be the other driver's fault. The car insurance rates went up because there had been accidents. Some of George's co-workers called him a "sucker" because he kept paying the higher rates. George paid for the insurance because he was afraid of being stuck with a large bill for personal damages if he didn't have insurance. He felt he had no power over Pete to force him to pay for the insurance. George cautioned Pete about driving while intoxicated and was told he had nothing to worry about. George felt uneasy about this, and he did feel he was a "sucker." But George did nothing about his feelings. When Pete was starting his senior year in high school he drove his car into a tree. He had some small cuts on his face. Fortunately, no one else had been in the car. Pete had obviously been drinking. Pete took a few swings at a policeman, but they were easily evaded because Pete had such poor balance at the time. The policeman gave Pete a ticket for driving under the influence of alcohol. He ignored Pete's feeble attempts at fighting because it was Pete's first offense and no one had been hurt. Pete refused any tests to determine if he had been drinking. Refusing the test in Pete's state usually led to an automatic driver's license suspension for six months. This was fine with Pete's parents, but Pete was furious. He told his grandparents that he had had only two beers and had refused the blood alcohol test because he was scared of needles. The grandparents convinced Pete's father to hire a lawyer for Pete. The lawyer was able to get the charges reduced to reckless driving. In this situation, Pete again used his grandparents to rescue him. In the past his grandparents had rescued him from consequences imposed by his parents. Now the outside world was being held off.

Pete's parents had long discussions about whether he should drive, get an allowance, do chores around the house, or be in by midnight. It really did not matter what they decided. Pete did as he pleased. Pete's parents did not recognize the anger they felt toward Pete. If they had been asked about it, they probably would have denied that they were angry with him. They certainly did not recognize the existence of many problems which would make most people angry. Pete's parents had a right to be angry at him. Until they were conscious of that anger, they would be unable to deal with him effectively. It is difficult to deal firmly with someone you care about unless you are angry with him; until anger is felt, it is difficult to impose painful consequences. Until Pete's parents felt anger, it would be difficult for them to let go.

THE POLICE FORCE A CRISIS

A few months after his car accident, Pete was caught selling marijuana. The defense lawyer kept Pete out of jail. However, his father had to pay a $500 fine and attorney fees, and Pete was put on probation for six months. The probation officer suggested that George and Mary attend a *Toughlove* meeting. They did, and discussed their problems during their first meeting. The parents in the group felt that Pete had used his parents as a doormat for too long. Both sets of grandparents had rescued Pete and had intimidated his parents, but the real problem was the parents' willingness to be abused. The group suggested that the *Toughlove* book be read and a plan for action be made.

Mary and George read the *Toughlove* book. Though it seemed impossible to arrange, they concluded that the only fair thing to do would be to ask Pete to pay the $500 fine and attorney fees. They also thought that Pete should stop using drugs and alcohol. There were other issues, but those seemed to be the most pressing and obvious. At the next *Toughlove* meeting they discussed their thoughts with the group. It was decided that another couple from the group would be present when George and Mary told Pete their demands.

When Pete was told he would have to get a job and pay back the $500 plus attorney fees, he started yelling. He threatened to quit school. He threatened to leave the state. He threatened to go live with his grandparents. Pete's parents were clearly intimidated. They wanted Pete to finish high school. They were fearful of losing his "love" and actual physical presence. They knew he was on parole and could not leave the state. They thought his grandparents would "spoil" him. The couple from the Toughlove group intervened and said, "Pete, it's your choice. You can quit school. You can leave the state. You can live anywhere someone will take you in. But if you want to live here, you will stop using drugs, stop drinking, and get a job to pay back the money you owe.

At that moment George and Mary realized they had failed to take a firm stand on many issues over the years. They had waited until Pete was almost finished with high school before taking a stand and making demands. They had been frightened, anxious, and angry with each other for years. Their marriage and the quality of their lives had deteriorated. And, none of it had helped Pete.

Taking a stand such as that suggested by the *Toughlove* parents would be appropriate for a seventeen-year-old such as Pete. Other stands and demands would be appropriate at other ages. However, taking a stand is no magic cure-all. Limits must be set and enforced. The teen must be dealt with in new and constantly changing situations. When a situation does not *feel* right, efforts must be made to find out why and how to correct the situation.

The books listed earlier in this chapter, and many others, deal exclusively with how to discipline and get along with children and teens. Consult them after you have finished this book.

Finding Your Feelings

Start focusing on your feelings about your own children. Answering the questions below might raise some issues relevant to your own situation.

1. Robert was not doing well in school. Robert's parents agreed to excuse him from his household chores if he improved his grades, even though Robert had plenty of free time. Were Robert's parents taking into account their own feelings and needs? Were they teaching Robert a way to escape his fair share of housework? Were they preventing Robert from learning how to enjoy successful accomplishment for its own sake?

2. Joy was always a few minutes late getting home at night. Her parents finally told her she would have to be in half an hour before the town's legal curfew, just to make sure she would be in on time. Joy did come home earlier, but "forgot" her key consistently, waking her parents at midnight several times. Joy's father was upset because he had to be up at 5 A.M. for his work. When questioned about her forgetfulness, Joy said it was difficult to remember because she was rushing all night to avoid coming home late. Joy's parents extended her curfew, and she started remembering her key. Had Joy's parents been manipulated? Did Joy feel much sympathy for her father when he was sleepy at work? What alternative actions could Joy's parents have taken?

3. Richard was in his first year of high school. He did barely passing work in school and never spent time on homework. Richard refused to do household chores. He was pleasant enough at home unless he was asked to do some work. He would refuse, politely at first. If pressured to do house or yard work, he would become angry and refuse to do it. His parents stopped his allowance, did not buy him new clothes, would not do his laundry for him, and refused to drive him anywhere. Richard wore his old clothes, did his own laundry at home, and spent most of his time with his friends. Richard spoke to his aunts and uncles in town about his lack of new clothes and an allowance. The relatives pressured Richard's parents to get him some nice clothes, "at least for church," and to give him an allowance. Were the relatives being rescuers? Did Richard's parents have the right to withhold new

clothes? Did Richard's parents have the right to be angry about Richard's refusal to do house or yard work?

4. Gary, sixteen years old, was arrested for using marijuana. The police asked his parents to take him home. Gary's father wanted him to spend a few days in jail as a "lesson." Gary's mother insisted on bailing him out immediately. Assuming the jail was clean and Gary had a private cell (was safe from harm from other prisoners): Would staying in jail be a worthwhile experience for Gary? Should Gary's parents bail him out? Would staying in jail teach Gary respect or fear for the law? Would any of these answers be different if Gary knew his parents also used illicit drugs?

Society, Personality
Growth, and
8 Letting Go

Parents who let go allow their teens to make their own decisions about how they will act. These parents also have enough self-confidence to institute consequences if the teen's behavior creates difficulties. Sometimes parents may disagree with a teen's behavior, but they are not particularly inconvenienced or injured by the behavior. In such cases, parents depend on society to provide consequences. The teen learns through experience how society will react to various behaviors.

For example, the teen may decide to neglect schoolwork or to stay out past curfew. Parents who let go will state their wishes, and then allow society to act. In this way, parents give the teen responsibility for making sure schoolwork is completed, hoping the school imposes effective consequences when schoolwork is poorly done. Parents count on society for imposing consistent, rational guidelines and consequences for teens, but in reality, many institutions in society fail to demand reasonable behavior from teens.

This chapter illustrates how various social institutions can fail to give teens useful feedback concerning their behavior. We'll see what actions you can take to encourage social institutions to deal more effectively with teens.

Society consists of school, mental health, religious, legal, and other systems. When feeling overwhelmed or intimidated by such systems, it is helpful to remember that society is nothing more than a large number of individuals. The "system" consists of individuals, some of whom do not care for the best interests of your adolescent.

Everyone does things at times because he or she thinks that

"society" would approve. A parent's perception of society is usually different than a teen's. It is useful to have these concepts in mind when considering how to interact with various elements in society. One cannot assume that the school, the police, a counselor, or the courts are always doing the right thing. After all, they are made up of people who are far from perfect.

The School System

LOVE OF LEARNING

One lesson schools could teach is how the real world works. In the real world, progress is acknowledged by rewards, status, and recognition. Failure is not rewarded in the real world. In school, however, students are often passed from one grade to another without learning how to read. Students may graduate from high school without having learned a minimum of material. When a student does not learn, the school often blames the parents, and the parents often blame the school. Failing a subject or a grade could teach a student that there are consequences of this action (or inaction). If a teen wants to learn, the school and the parents will each find it easier to help the teen learn. If the teen does not want to learn, the consequences of having to repeat courses and not being able to get a job may be necessary to change the teen's attitude.

In some cases teachers will lay a guilt trip on parents, saying they should help the teen to study. For example, Bert's geometry teacher called Bert's mother and told her to make sure Bert did his homework. The teacher accused Bert's mother of not caring about his schoolwork. Bert's mother told the teacher that it was the school's responsibility to check homework. Bert's mother promised not to complain if Bert was kept late for extra instruction, got poor grades, or even had to repeat a class because of poor work. She made it clear that it was up to the school to let Bert know how poorly he was doing, and that it was up to Bert to decide what to do about it. Parents who let go will not give in to such accusations. When your teen does poorly in a course, try to help the teen and the school interact effectively.

Ask the teacher to provide your teen with help in learning. At the same time let the teacher know that if your teen gets a poor grade or does not pass, you will not complain or blame the school because you understand that the teen is responsible for the poor grades. Do not nag the teen about studying. Do not pay the teen money for good grades. Let go by allowing the teen to take responsibility and pride in work well done; your teen may begin to enjoy learning. Do not get into arguments and power struggles concerning study time, homework, and grades. Let the teen deal with the real world.

Many parents would shudder at the thought of allowing their child to choose to do poorly in school. After all, if a child is not prepared for and does not do well in high school, it will not be possible to get into a good college or get a good job. Many parents feel that children should not be allowed to make such costly, permanent, harmful mistakes. We believe that the teen who is reminded and pushed to do homework will learn to hate it and will develop poor study and work habits. When the teen gets a job or gets into college, the ability to make decisions and work independently will have to be acquired under even more pressing circumstances.

EXPELLING STUDENTS

Some schools expel students as punishment for misbehavior: the student must stay away from the school for a number of days and cannot make up the missed work. This system places the misbehaving teen at home with his or her parents. Thus, schools shirk their responsibility toward the teen and throw it back to the parents. If the parents work, the teen is alone at home...on vacation! The "punishment" of getting out of school is not a painful one, unless the teen cares about grades. Missing school is likely to bring academic failure unless the student is very strong academically to start with. If your teen is expelled, make an objection. Tell the school that you would be happy to have your teen stay late, do extra book reports, or sweep the school floors as recompense, BUT you do not want your teen out of school. Perhaps a detention room is needed: students could be made to sit in a room for an hour after school and be allowed to do their homework or extra academic work. Take your complaints to the school board if necessary. Force the system to become accountable.

CRIME IN THE SCHOOLS

Illegal student activities are sometimes not reported to the police by teachers, even when school policy dictates that reports should be made. Failure to bring consequences for illegal activities show students (and their friends) that it is possible to get away with such activities. Wrong-doing may not be reported for a variety of reasons: it is time-consuming to deal with problems; the teacher wants to be popular (or at least avoid trouble); or the teacher does not see the activity as being really serious, as in the case of certain drugs that are not considered too bad because "everyone is smoking pot these days."

Parents also often wish to prevent their teens from experiencing really effective consequences. Many, if not most parents would prefer to be told about their teen's drug use or schoolyard fighting rather than have the police called into the matter. When school officials and other persons choose not to report problems in your teen's school, you might consider reporting the situation yourself or insisting that the school do so.

There are three questions to consider when trying to decide if the police should or should not be called in when illegal activities are discovered at school:

1. Do you want the job of choosing and enforcing the consequences your teen is to receive?

2. Do you want your teen to learn that illegal activities will bring no police action?

3. If the activity was done by your teen or by other students, will the activity continue without effective limits?

MATURING GRADUALLY

Many parents feel that their kids are just going through a stage, that the kids will straighten out when they "grow up." Parents naturally want to protect their kids from painful consequences. Parents will take harmful substances from the mouth of a baby and spend hundreds of hours reading and explaining things to the child, but the same parents may not see that the child will have to face consequences for taking drugs or throwing away educational opportunities during the teen years.

One gradually loses control over various aspects of a child's life. It takes several years for a teen to learn how to take control of his or her self. If the teen is allowed to feel the consequences of past mistakes, there is a greater chance of intelligent decisions being made in the future. A teen will learn little from experience if his or her parents argue with teachers about grades, pay a lawyer to have deserved charges dismissed, and otherwise keep the teen from feeling the consequences of his actions.

Randy, for example, made it through high school fairly easily.

During his first semester in college, Randy partied. He did not study because he had never had trouble passing high school courses. He failed all his final examinations. Randy's parents told him they had wasted enough money on college. He was on his own. Randy found a job in a factory, but was not satisfied with the work. He worked part-time, paid his own tuition, and eventually finished college. His parents motivated him more by letting go than by paying his way to college.

The Legal System

As described in the chapter on legal issues, the legal system is constantly changing. Laws, precedents, and practices vary almost from day to day in any given city. Juvenile laws are open to much interpretation and variability in application. Status offenses (actions which are crimes only because they were done by a minor, such as curfew violations) are often not acted upon by prosecutors. Nevertheless, continued violations can be one sign of an out-of-control teen.

Juvenile offenses often carry no permanent criminal record. The criteria for a juvenile court disposition often comes down to what is best for the minor's best interests. For example, a prescription for counseling might be considered appropriate for some offenses. This may be ineffective if the teen is already in counseling or is not motivated for counseling. Work programs and the order to compensate the victim of a crime may be ineffective if probation is not enforced. Probation officers are often too busy to monitor the minor who has been found guilty of status offenses.

In some jurisdictions parents cannot ask for court help in controlling their children because of juvenile statutes that are ineffective or not enforced. Statutes that can help parents use the force of the legal system to control their teens include the Minor Requiring Authoritative Intervention Act, the Persons in Need of Supervision Act, and other similar acts.

When police and courts don't enforce consequences for lawbreaking minors who are beyond their parent's control, teens learn they can break the law. This is an unrealistic lesson. If a family can work out its problems, that's great. However, what often happens is that the teen continues to be an offender, and the court waits for counseling to work. Finally, the minor runs away, gets involved in drugs, and ultimately the court does get involved — when the teen commits a serious crime. Similarly, teens learn disrespect for the legal system when there are no consequences for failing to report to probation officers. In one area the Juvenile Court probation officer would report teens who failed to appear to the State's Attorney. The State's Attorney did nothing about these cases.

Teens are very aware of laws and of how well they are enforced. For example, in our area the high school truancy rate was twelve percent until a judge started putting students in the detention center for repeated truancy. The truancy rate fell to three percent. When a change in the law prevented continued court action, the truancy rate returned to twelve percent.

WHAT TO DO

It is difficult to fight City Hall. It takes years to change laws. What you can do is attempt to bring effective consequences to your teen under the existing laws. It is also important to bring consequences to those who are getting your teen into trouble. If your teen is breaking the law, make sure the police know about those who led your teen into trouble. Find out who is selling illegal drugs and which bars or adults are serving minors. Let the police know when and where the action is taking place. If your teen has been accused of some crime, let the attorneys and court know that it would be in the teen's best interest to order counseling *and* some real consequences. If the teen fails to cooperate with counseling and succeeds at ignoring work orders, let the parole officer know about it. Bring the problems to the court's attention. Push the system by demanding accountability.

The Mental Health and Counseling System

There are many counselors available to help you and your teen. Counselors differ in their educational backgrounds, beliefs, experiences, available time, goals, and abilities. Which counselor is best depends on your situation.

A school counselor might be most familiar with school requirements and peer group characteristics. A clinical social worker, psychiatrist, or psychologist might be best at recognizing teens with serious emotional problems or mental illness.

Sometimes more than one counselor will be needed: a physician might test for physical problems, while a social worker gives counseling. One teen carried this to an extreme. She had a county mental health social worker, a counselor from a runaway shelter, and two high school counselors all concerned about her case. She was having conversations with several of these people each day. Most of them were convinced she was being mistreated by her parents. Actually her parents were getting tough with her by enforcing some consequences. A meeting of all the counselors with the teen's mother cleared up the problem when inconsistencies in the teen's stories were found. The meeting, by the way, was initiated by the teen's mother when she found out how many counselors her teen was giving her sad story to.

This teen's parents did have some changes to make in the way they were relating to their daughter. However, the mental health system wanted to keep hearing the daughter's victim story. If you find a counselor who keeps excusing your teen's behavior and attempting to portray the teen as a helpless victim, then find a new counselor, but you must objectively consider the teen's complaints to see if you are being neglectful in some way. In any case, it is likely that the whole family needs to make some changes in the way they relate to each other. The whole family's pain needs to be heard, but limits have to be set on the teen's acting-out behavior. Don't accept blame from a counselor for your teen's inappropriate behavior. Don't accept the statement that he is taking drugs, for example, because you won't hear his needs. This is disrespectful of you and of your teen. You are responsible for hearing your teen's feelings. The teen is responsible for how he or she expresses those feelings.

Another teen had a problem with drug usage. Her experiences show that even when help is needed, counselors and others can each fail in their own way to do any good. Sometimes parents have to define what they can tolerate and take matters in their own hands. One teacher refused to report the teen for using drugs, saying it would be unfair to do so because "everyone was using them." The parents asked a policeman to talk to the teen about drugs. The teen got a lecture on abortion. A physician saw the teen and prescribed antidepressants, which the parents did not understand. A psychologist saw the teen and was convinced that she was not taking any drugs. When some teachers found that the teen was going to get drug counseling at an agency, they recommended against it, saying that it would ruin her future and she would never be able to get a government job. Though the teen denied taking any, a drug testing service did detect drugs in the teen's blood. The teen was

put into a drug abuse program, which did help. The mother succeeded in getting help for the teen, but in the process had to reject
the advice of teachers, a physician, and several counselors.

Drugs, Alcohol, and Society

The confusion and uncertainty in society concerning drugs and
alcohol is a more pressing problem today than it was in the 1950's.
It has been said for many years that alcohol and cigarettes may be
legal, but they have caused more deaths and disease than marijuana, cocaine, and heroin. So why should these other drugs be
illegal? Isn't society being hypocritical? This argument still stands
as well as ever but is more troublesome now because all these drugs
are so easily available to youngsters today. It is true that smoking
kills 1,000 Americans daily, and automobile accidents due to
alcohol kill nearly 100 Americans a day. Still, that does not make
illicit drugs good, or even tolerable.

WHAT TO DO

Recognize that tobacco, cocaine, and alcohol are each multi-
billion dollar industries. While social and political action against
these industries are needed, such actions are not likely to bring
results quickly enough to help you and your teen. Steps you can
take include:

1. Discuss the situation with your teen. Offer professional help
if there is real addiction present. Visit agencies and programs in or
near your community which specialize in substance abuse.

2. If you have values that would be offended by drinking or
drug use in your home, tell your teen you will not tolerate such
behavior in the house. If your teen is intoxicated, provide a sleeping bag in the back yard, assuming it is safe to sleep there. Otherwise, attempt to secure reasonable temporary housing elsewhere,
as in a detoxification center. Cut off allowance and other
sources of money.

3. Inform the police of sources of drugs and alcohol. Do so
anonymously, as drug dealers are not always understanding or
forgiving.

4. Destroy any illegal drugs you find...flush them down the
toilet. Let your teen know you are going to do this ahead of time.
One warning is sufficient. Follow it with periodic inspections.

5. If your teen becomes violent, call the police.

Society and You

A look at society will show that it is made of many separate individuals. No matter what you do, you cannot please everyone. You cannot please very many people, in fact. You can only do what is right for you and your teen. If you are unsuccessful in pleasing or being able to help your teen, you may only be able to help yourself. Sometimes a teen benefits most when parents let go of the teen's problems. Then the teen is exposed to natural consequences and has a chance to help himself or herself. Hopefully the school, mental health, and legal systems which are part of our society will provide teens with effective lessons. When parents let go it becomes important that children can bump into rational consequences that are provided by an enlightened society.

This book has discussed many ways you can develop personally. Parents are often forced to mature when their teens rebel. Parents may come to question their old ways of dealing with life, and their purpose in life. They question their values and their happiness. When teens are no longer cute and compliant little children, parents often must look to themselves for enjoyment and fulfillment. At the same time parents are forced to let go of their children, they can get a hold on their own lives.

Ideally, society should deal thoughtfully and rationally with your teen once you let go. As this chapter suggests, unfortunately, this isn't always the case!

9.

Legal Aspects of Letting Go

Much has been written about the legal rights of children and teens; such information is needed and useful. However, there is a distinct lack of information concerning the legal rights of parents. One recent book that explains many of the legal rights of parents states: "The rights of parents to our knowledge...have never been explained before." (Alan Sussman and Martin Guggenheim, The Rights of Parents.) In contrast, there are thousands of books, articles, and agencies concerned with the legal rights of children and teens.

This chapter describes some of the legal rights and responsibilities of parents. We will discuss parental liability for the acts of teens, control and discipline of teens, the rights of relatives, teenage marriage, medical care, and alcohol and drugs.

The Law Changes

The law changes when new laws are passed and when courts make new decisions. The laws concerning teens (and many other topics) vary from state to state and even from city to city. The interpretation and application of laws may vary from day to day in any given city, depending on the school official, policeman, or judge applying the law. The information given in this chapter is based upon: 1) the 1985 *Illinois Revised Statutes*, 2) *The Rights of Parents* (Sussman and Guggenheim, 1980), and 3) our observations that have come through our professional experiences.

127

The Rights of Parents

CUSTODY

Perhaps the most universal and best-recognized right of parents is the right to the custody of their children. The right of parents to maintain control and custody of their children prevails in the face of difficult economic conditions and psychological problems.

If your teen has been consistently in trouble, you may not consider the right to "keep" your teen to be a valuable treasure. This may not seem to be one of the legal rights you wanted to hear about. However, it can be an advantage when dealing with outside influences on your teen. For example, if your teen wishes to dodge household chores and other conditions you have imposed by going to live with Aunt Tillie, you can demand that your teen live with you. You do have the right to protect your teen from religious cults, relatives, and others who might try to make your teen leave home. You do not have to bargain, make deals, or give concessions to keep your teen at home. The police and courts will recognize and help enforce your right to keep your teen at home.

If your teen has been threatening to move in with a neighbor or relative, you have the right to veto the move. You have the right to stand firm and not be manipulated. Counseling is not necessarily indicated, as it would be for the teen who plans to run away to live on the road. If your teen threatens to move in with a friend or relative, simply say, "If you go to live there or anywhere else, I will have the police bring you back home. It is my responsibility to provide you with a safe home. You will stay here and follow the rules." There is no need to give your teen an allowance, excuse him or her from chores, or do anything else to keep him or her at home. It is your legal right to demand that your teen live at home.

If relatives or friends are keeping your teen at their home, ask an attorney what charges could be brought in your area. In most states a minor is anyone under eighteen years of age, though for various purposes the age may be different. In some areas it is a crime to harbor a minor against the parents' wishes.

What is legally possible may not be most practical or the best course of action. For example, by insisting that your teen return to your home, you may cause your teen to move farther away. Whether or not one should threaten (or carry out threats against) others depends on the situation. If a friendly relative is keeping your teen safe and in school, a cooling-off period might do

everyone some good. While it would be "legal" to force the teen to
return to your home, the teen might benefit more by living with
others and perhaps gain perspective on your home situation.

About two million American children and teens do run away
from home each year. This is not to be encouraged or taken lightly.
The teen or child who runs away to live on the street or to "make it
on his or (her) own" is going into a physically and economically difficult situation. This is different than a move to a friend's or relative's
home. If your teen has run away and come back, or if you believe
your teen may run away, professional counseling *is* needed.

Some adults, including a small minority of those who work at
shelters for runaways and other social institutions, will believe
untrue stories told by teens who wish to leave home for a short
while. These people may be manipulated; they may be convinced
to give the teen a place to stay, rather than leave the teen at home
where problems (and you) must be dealt with.

Teens can use a runaway shelter as a rescuing service. The law
usually requires that you be notified if your teen goes to a shelter.
You can tell the shelter that you are not giving permission for your
teen to leave home. Runaway shelters frequently deal with teens
from severely dysfunctional families with sexual and physical
abuse and economic and emotional neglect. You may, therefore, be
greeted initially with distrust. An angry teen who is furious at your
new rules may give a very biased story of your intentions and conditions at home. People at the shelter may be taken in by the teen's
stories of these bad conditions.

For example, one teen told a school social worker that he wanted to be put in a runaway shelter because his home was
unsanitary...there was rotting food on the floors, bugs and mice
crawling around, and his father was drunk all the time. In fact, none
of this was true. The social worker called the teen's father to say
that a report of child neglect was going to be filed with the local
authorities. The teen's father said that he knew it was the social
worker's responsibility to report all suspected cases of abuse or
neglect. He also asked that the social worker come to his home that
day to see what the situation really was and to discuss problems the
teen was having. When the social worker came to the home it was
clear that none of the charges were true and that the father was
very concerned about his son. In going over the teen's school
records it was discovered that there were several excuses for missing classes which the teen had written out himself, signing his
father's name. The father encouraged the school social worker to

give the teen the usual consequences the school prescribed for such behavior. The father was not manipulated by his teen's threats of leaving home. Instead, the father took a strong stand and obtained help from the agency the teen had tried to turn against him. It should be remembered that counselors do see many children and teens who have been abused by their parents. Counselors have a moral and legal obligation to report even suspected cases. If the anger level in your home has gotten so high that you have abused your child, you should seek professional help.

DISCIPLINE

Parents have the right to discipline their children. The law recognizes the right of parents to spank, but not physically injure their children. Unfortunately, by the teen years spankings have become ineffective. Parents have the right to impose curfews on their children, but do not have the right to lock their children in a closet: common sense is behind most of the laws that dictate what is reasonable behavior for parents. However, some teens do not behave reasonably when it comes to curfew and other items.

When teen behavior involves breaking the law, as with curfew or school truancy, it is usually best to let the teen deal with the authorities. The parent can be interested in the teen's problems and, at the same time, let the police or school officials know that the teen is responsible for breaking the law. In reality, status offenses (acts which are illegal only when committed by a minor) are rarely enforced by the police unless the parents insist. Some teens find they can get their parents to write excuses for missing school and have their parents assure the police that curfew will not be violated in the future, thus getting the teen off the hook. Free yourself (let go) of responsibility for acts committed by your teen. It is often better to let the teen suffer whatever consequences the system has in store. It is better for the teen to get a juvenile record (which is not permanent in many states) than to continue to break the law because of lack of consequences.

Many attorneys have great disdain for status offenses. An attorney may attempt to have such charges dropped because of a lack of faith in the juvenile justice system to change the teen's future behavior. Having charges dropped may not be harmful if the teen does receive some sort of therapy and/or consequence. However, in some cases all a teen learns from such an encounter with the law is that a "good" lawyer can get charges dropped.

When parents find themselves unsuccessful in controlling

their teen's extreme acting-out behavior, they may ask the state to help control the teen. All states have laws that enable juvenile courts to exercise control over children who are not being controlled by their parents (Sussman and Guggenheim). These laws are sometimes called Children in Need of Supervision (CHINS) or Persons in Need of Supervision (PINS) statutes. The state can help the parent discipline the teen, or in certain cases, take the teen from the parents by court order, placing the teen in a detention center or foster home. Parents may be required to financially support such arrangements. Separating the teen from his or her parents is often accomplished with great difficulty, even when the parents are in favor of it.

MARRIAGE AND THE MILITARY

In most states, teens cannot marry or join the military without written permission from their parents. This is generally true until the age of eighteen.

LOSS OF PARENTAL RIGHTS

There are three ways parental rights can be terminated (Sussman and Guggenheim). First, when a child reaches the age of majority, usually age eighteen, parental rights are terminated. It is interesting to observe the behavior of "young men" in their twenties who are still living with (or supported by) their parents, not working and not going to school. Some of these young men fit the pattern described in *The Peter Pan Syndrome* by Dan Kiley, Ph.D. Although they may legally be adults, these young Peter Pans are still in NeverNever Land. Some of these young men have problems with repeated automobile accidents associated with drunk driving.

The second way parental rights can be terminated is by a court ruling. This can occur when children are neglected or abused. The third way parental rights can be lost is through emancipation of the child. Emancipation can lead to loss of some or all parental rights and responsibilities. Laws concerning emancipation vary from state to state. Children ay become emancipated if they marry, join the armed forces, become parents, or live by themselves without financial assistance.

If you cannot control your teen and living with him or her is extremely difficult, you may want to find out what is required to have the teen declared emancipated or a minor in need of supervision. The age and wishes of the teen affect the possibility of early emancipation, which is usually a difficult process involving a lawyer's assistance.

LIVING AWAY FROM HOME AGAINST THE PARENTS' WISHES

Parents can usually veto a minor teen's move from home. If a teen does move from home against parental wishes, the parents are no longer required to financially support the teen. As long as a teen is living at home, parents are required to provide adequate food, shelter, and clothing. However, teens do not have the right to move out against the wishes of their parents and continue to demand financial support.

The Law and Education

Most parents are quite concerned about the education of their children. Children today are given calculators, computers, digital watches, and other complex devices. Some of us who grew up in the 1950's were fascinated by static electricity, light bulbs, and the magic of television picture. Science was interesting. Now, science is taken for granted by many people. It is difficult to develop curiosity about how something works when it is commonplace. When one is surrounded by video games, computers, and space shuttles, one may cease to appreciate them. It is the new and usual that is perceived as interesting. Actually one of us (R.F.) was recently asked a question by an eight-year-old about the functioning of a television. Upon seeing our black and white television, he said, "What's wrong with your TV? It seems to have lost its color."

The natural wonder associated with some school subjects has become blunted. In addition, some traditional reasons for seeking an education have been obscured for many. In generations past, memory of the Depression or fear of the military draft kept students in school with at least passing grades. Now many students feel that they will be provided for whether or not they obtain marketable skills. And perhaps they are right.

Parents often feel responsible for the education of their children and teens. Even without the modern "excuses" for not being interested in education listed above, it has always been true that many students were not enthusiastic about school. When a child or teen understands that an issue is important to his or her parents, that topic can become the basis for a power struggle.

Power Struggle

Children and teens can try quite a few tricks to make their parents worry about school, education, truancy, and related issues. Some parents are simply concerned that their children are not doing well or may not get into the best college. Other parents are concerned that they will be held responsible for their children's truancy and other school problems. Almost all states have compulsory education laws which require children to obtain an education until the age of sixteen or seventeen. In many states, home study, private, or religious schools are legal alternatives. If parents do not allow their children to attend school, they can be charged with neglect. Parents should provide their teens with the opportunity to go to school (an alarm clock and bus money). If the teen fails to get to school, the school system will hopefully put pressure on the teen long before the parents are charged with responsibility for lateness or truancy. As with most teen issues, GIVE ASSISTANCE ONLY WHEN IT IS NEEDED. For example, your teen may have "trouble waking up in time for school." On some days your teen may be too tired to go to school.

Take Roger, for instance. He started to sleep later and later. His mother had to try a little harder each day to wake him. After a while, Roger was missing the school bus, and his mother was driving him to school almost every day. After talking to some neighbors, Roger's mother decided that she had had enough of waking and driving Roger. She told him that she would not wake him, give him rides, or give him excuses for being late to school. The next day Roger claimed he was sick...he had the flu...his stomach hurt. His mother said she would excuse him from school if he stayed in bed all day. That afternoon Roger was out playing ball. His mother refused to write an excuse note for him. She stopped taking responsibility for him. She LET GO. Roger had to serve several detentions for missing school that day and for coming late to school on several other days. His mother had a lot more time in the mornings after that.

SEX, VD, AND MEDICAL TREATMENT

Laws concerning sex education in schools and medical treatment for sexual problems are changing. Medical treatment as it relates to venereal disease, abortion, and pregnancy prophylaxis is a controversial and complex subject.

Many teens (and sometimes their parents) are unaware of basic medical facts related to sex, pregnancy, and venereal disease. One study showed that about fifty percent of teenage girls (and ten percent of their mothers) did not know that intercourse caused pregnancy!

Many teens have gonorrhea and other infections. They continue to spread these infections rather than being checked and treated for them periodically. Gonorrhea and chlamydia are vaginal infections which women can carry for months or years before the infections cause problems. If the fifteen- to nineteen-year age group, about two percent of sexually active women have a flare-up of one of these infections each year (David A. Eschenbach, "New Concepts of Obstetric and Gynecologic Infection," Archives of Internal Medicine). The flare-up is referred to as PID. When there is a flare-up, infection spreads to the Fallopian tubes, giving a tubal infection, or PID, (Pelvic Inflammatory Disease). In the United States there are 42,000 teens (aged fifteen to nineteen) hospitalized each year for PID. Another 158,000 are treated as outpatients (Eugene A. Washington, Peter S. Arno, and Marie A. Brooks, "The Economic Costs of Pelvic Inflammatory Disease," Journal of the American Medical Association). These infections cause scarring of the tubes, leading to permanent infertility in some cases. Another problem caused by scarred tubes is ectopic pregnancy, a condition which affects about 4,100 teens each year. In ectopic pregnancy the fertilized egg gets caught in the scarred Fallopian tube, leading to the growth of the fetus there. The baby eventually dies, sometimes causing bleeding which is fatal for the mother as well.

PID can cause chronic pelvic pain, recurrent infections, and infertility. The following table from Eschenbach (1982) lists some of the consequences of PID.

Consequences of PID (tubal infection)	Frequency, %
Chronic pain 15 Subsequent PID	20-25 Infertility
1 infection	10-15
2 infections	25-35
3 infections	50-75
Ectopic pregnancy	7
(with first subsequent pregnancy)	

Many teens are several months into their pregnancy before they realize they are pregnant. This eliminates the possibility of proper prenatal care. For those teens who would want one, this also eliminates the possibility of an early abortion. At any time during pregnancy the law will not allow an abortion to be performed on a teen who does not want it...the parents' wishes do not override the teen's.

Because of the widespread lack of information and the widespread presence of venereal infections and teen pregnancies, some high schools have begun to teach sex education, give out birth control pills, and provide day care for children of high school students. Often there is opposition to sex education and these other actions. However, many parents do realize that a teen who knows the dangers of sexual activity might try to avoid the real problems that intercourse can bring.

Secret Treatment

In many states it is possible for teens to obtain treatment for VD without the knowledge or permission of their parents. It can be argued that parents could obtain counseling and other help for their teens if they knew about their medical conditions and infections. It could also be argued that the teen has a right to confidentiality...and might not seek treatment if confidentiality were not guaranteed. In some areas teens can obtain prophylactic drugs or devices and even abortions without the knowledge or consent of their parents. The legal, moral, and ethical questions associated with these issues have no clear answer. The laws are changing, making what is legally "right" or "wrong" change with time.

If sexual activity is a problem with your teen, professional counseling might be indicated, even before trouble is clearly present. Sexual activity can lead to pregnancy and a variety of dangerous and incurable infections. As with drunk driving, parents are often unable to shield their teens from the natural consequences of sexual activity. Getting adequate factual information to teens about sex is vital. The consequences of sexual intercourse are so great that parents must *not* let go before providing teens with enough information to make intelligent decisions.

For example, as this is being written, an unmarried seventeen-year-old girl is being admitted to the hospital. She did not know she was pregnant until today. Careful questioning about her menstrual periods and symptoms led to the conclusion that she was three or four months pregnant, and her bag of waters (amniotic fluid sac) ruptured several days ago. Since then she has had pain and fever: there is infection in her uterus. Her unborn baby is dead. This teen stands a good chance of needing a hysterectomy. She has some chance of dying from the infection. According to her father, this teen had regularly avoided the consequences associated with not doing homework or schoolwork. However, it may not be possible to save her from the consequences of her gonorrhea and other infections.

In theory, if children and teens are made to take responsibility for their actions on small items, they may learn to be responsible when more serious problems come along. However, many teens do not learn to take responsibility, not matter how hard their parents try to allow them to take the natural consequences that come with daily problems. In such cases, parents need not feel guilty or shamed when their teens suffer the medical effects of sexual activity.

Sexual activity is an example of an area in which parents may have little control over their teens. Though parents may tell their teens it is wrong, immoral, and dangerous to engage in sexual activity, the influence of society and other teens can be over-powering. In the early 1980's, I (R.F.) interviewed for a position as a physician at a college health center. I had heard from physicians in town that the students thought little of the quality of care given by the health center. And, perhaps they were right. The physicians I spoke to in that community had seen improperly sutured wounds, missed fractures, and other examples of poor care from the health center. As part of my interview at the college health center, a group of students interviewed me. These were mostly female college students. They did not ask me about my training or my ability to suture, detect fractures, or recognize diseases. Instead, I was quizzed about my ability to fit diaphragms, willingness to give out birth control pills, and about my "open-mindedness" when treating venereal diseases. In such school environments it is likely that many teens, regardless of what their parents have taught them, will become sexually active. Pregnancy may occur. Venereal infections will be caught, often with permanent consequences. Parents cannot always prevent their teens from becoming sexually active, for society and peers have great influence. Parents need to LET GO of the idea that they should feel guilty or responsible when their teens become pregnant or contract venereal disease.

Many parents raise their unmarried teen's children, especially if it allows the teen to finish school or hold a job. This rescues the teen from many of the consequences of having a baby, but may in the long run be desirable if it allows the teen to finish school. This is a difficult decision for the surprised grandparent. The decision concerning whether or not to raise a grandchild may best be reached with the help òf a counselor or religious clergy.

ALCOHOL AND OTHER DRUGS

The national statistics have said for years that about half of the 50,000 Americans killed in automobile accidents yearly died in accidents due to alcohol. Many more people are injured than are killed. Working in a hospital emergency department makes one think that the fifty percent figure is low...it seems that most serious accidents have alcohol involved. In many cases, there is no testing for the presence of alcohol. Even if alcohol was obviously involved, it may not be reported by a physician because it might prevent insurance payments from being made. In other cases it is felt the person with a wrecked car and physical injuries has had enough "punishment" without being charged with drunk driving.

Parents sometimes fail to note that their teens are using drugs or alcohol. Alcohol is usually the easiest drug to recognize because of its odor. Alcohol and marijuana each can cause loss of short-term memory: the person may forget what has been said from one minute to the next. Judgment and physical coordination are also impaired.

Actions You Can Take

Alcohol and drug abuse are serious problems for people of all ages in our society today. If your teen is using drugs or drinking alcohol, professional counseling is needed. If your teen drinks even a little on dates and drives, you can expect a serious accident.

IF YOUR TEEN USES DRUGS OR DRINKS ALCOHOL WHEN DRIVING, TRY TO PREVENT YOUR TEEN FROM DRIVING.

Riding with other drunk drivers is also unsafe. It may be that your teen owns a car or motorcycle, and you are not in control of his or her actions. However, the least you can do is not lend your car, not pay for gas, and cut off the teen's supply of money which might be used for drugs. This would include not giving an allowance. Do not leave credit cards, checks, or money lying around. Tell relatives not to give the teen money. While parents cannot control their teens completely, these measures may help. Too often parents provide the means for disaster, as when they buy a car or motorcycle for a teen who is known to drink occasionally. Many fatal crashes seem to occur soon after a teen has been given a car.

In addition to the usual methods of discipline, what can be done legally to discourage teen drinking and drug use? There are several things you can do.

Legal Actions to Stop Drug and Alcohol Abuse

1. It is legal for you to inspect your teen's room and confiscate any drugs or alcohol you find.

2. It is legal for you to ask that the school inspect your teen's locker, or (preferably) the locker of whomever is supplying drugs to your teen.

3. You can charge (or threaten to charge) adults who give your teen liquor with contributing to the delinquency of a minor and supplying liquor to a minor. "Men" in their early 20's as well as older teens, often supply younger teens with liquor and drugs.

4. You can have the police inspect ID's ("raid") at a bar that caters to teens.

Responsibility for the Acts of Your Teen

Parents often wonder if they will be held responsible for the acts of their children or teens. These days it seems that everyone is suing everybody for everything. So, anything is possible. For example, a Florida court ruled that a parent may be liable to others for letting a five-year-old ride a bicycle. the case came up when the child hit a woman on a sidewalk (Sussman and Guggenheim) in a case involved the Southern American Fire Insurance Company v. Maxwell (Fla., 1973).

In general, one could expect to be held liable for act of children which were somewhat predictable or "foreseeable," Leaving a loaded gun where young children might get to it could be expected to lead to trouble. As another example, if parents know their child is likely to hurt others because of some psychological problem, professional help should be sought. Call your local community mental health center and seek help for the teen. Fear of retaliation by mentally-troubled teens often prevents parents from getting teens much-needed help.

If a child is acting as an employee of his or her parents, the parents are liable for the acts of the child, as they would be for the acts of any employee.

Beyond the above-mentioned theories of liability, some states have passed laws making parents financially liable for willful acts of their children that cause damage or injury to others. Parents are required to pay even if they had no way of knowing their child was likely to commit the act. Such laws have been enacted to try to reduce juvenile crime by encouraging parents to control their children's behavior. Most of these laws limit parental liability to a certain amount, such as $1,000 (Sussman and Guggenheim).

Conclusions

This book has touched on many areas of the parent-teen letting go process. There are multiple factors that influence this sometimes difficult parent-teen transitional time. Some of these influences include the parent's own childhood, the parent's reactions to aging, and the teen's reactions to his or her own development. Complicating this process even further is the fact that social institutions also have an impact on family life and the separation process. The legal system, school system, and various other agencies may all have some bearing on parent-teen relations. No wonder this is a difficult time for both parent and teen!

Life with a teen also drives home one very hard fact — the only person you can truly control is yourself. If life hasn't taught that lesson, then parenting a teen hopefully will. During the separation stage of adolescence, parents may feel a loss of control in the area of supervising their child's life. Still, another opportunity awaits the parents — the opportunity to focus on their own growth and personal development.

What constitutes being a "good parent" changes with the child's developmental stage. This crisis of family transition forces parents to reevaluate what their parental role is, as well as what changes they would like to make in their own lives. A crisis can be a frightening time because everything may seem so uncertain. If your primary identity has revolved around parenting, this can be an especially frightening time. You may be asking questions like the following: "Who am I now?" "Where should I put my time?" "How do I deal with the scary feelings of abandonment and loss?" Your teen is probably dealing with similar questions and anxieties. It is not an easy process; but letting go appropriately can be a tremendous gift for your teen, giving him or her the chance to develop more independence and responsibility. Letting go, as we have tried to relate, can also be a tremendous gift to your own self-development as well. Good Luck!

Appendix:
Reference Sources

Bernstein, Jerrold G.: "Kids and Drugs," *Drug Therapy*, March, 1984, pp. 193-208.

Bloom, Michael V.: *Adolescent-Parental Separation.* Gardner Press, New York, 1980.

Dinkmeyer, Don and McKay, Gary D.: *Step-Teen: Systematic Training for Effective Parenting of Teens.* American Guidance Service, Circle Pines, MN, 1983.

Esenbach, David A.: "New Concepts of Obstetric and Gynecologic Infection," *Archives of Internal Medicine*, vol. 142, October 25, 1982, pp. 2039-2044.

Fiumara, Nicholas J.: "Treating Gonorrhea," *American Family Physician*, May, 1981, pp. 123-126.

Garner, Al: "Parents Need to Let Go of Mentally Disturbed Offspring," *American Medical News*, April 11, 1986, p. 56.

Halpern, Howard M.: *How to Break Your Addiction to a Person.* Bantam Books, New York, 1982.

Kiley, Dan: *Keeping Kids Out of Trouble* (Originally, *Nobody Said It Would Be Easy*). Warner Books, New York, 1978.

Morganthau, Tom; Miller, Mark; Huck, Janet; and DeQuine, Jeanne: "Kids and Cocaine," *Newsweek*, March 17, 1986, pp. 58-65.

Mussen, Paul Henry; Conger, John Janeway; and Kagan, Jerome: *Child Development and Personality*, Fourth Edition. Harper & Row, New York, 1974.

National Association of Social Workers: "At Life's End, Looking Back Building Legacy," *NASW News*, September, 1985, p. 3.

Quinn, William H.; Newfield, Neal A.; and Protinsky, Howard O.: "Rites of Passage in Families with Adolescents," *Family Process*, vol. 24, March 1985, pp. 101-111.

Schachter, Julius: "Sexually Transmitted Chlamydia Trachomatis Infection, Management of the Most Common Venereal Disease," *Postgraduate Medicine*, vol. 72, no. 4, October, 1982, pp. 60-69.

Sussman, Alan and Guggenheim, Martin: *The Rights of Parents*, An American Civil Liberties Union Handbook. Avon Books, 1980.

Wanderer, Zev and Cabot, Tracy: *Letting Go: How to Survive a Lost Romance — and Make Your New Love Life Better!* Warner Books, New York, 1978.

Washington, A. Eugene; Arno, Peter S.; and Brooks, Marie A.: "The Economic Cost of Pelvic Inflammatory Disease," *Journal of the American Medical Association*, April 4, 1986, vol. 255, no. 13, pp. 1735-1737.

York, Phyllis and David; and Wachtel, Ted: *Toughlove*. Bantam Books, New York, 1982.

York, Phyllis and David: *Toughlove Cocaine: Help for People Who Care About a Cocaine User*. Toughlove, P.O. Box 1069, Doylestown, PA 18901, The Toughlove Press, 1985.

Index